EASY PIANO

Jazz Songs
FOR KIDS

ISBN 978-1-70516-537-9

HAL•LEONARD®

Visit Hal Leonard Online at
www.halleonard.com

World headquarters, contact:
Hal Leonard
7777 West Bluemound Road
Milwaukee, WI 53213
Email: info@halleonard.com

In Europe, contact:
Hal Leonard Europe Limited
1 Red Place
London, W1K 6PL
Email: info@halleonardeurope.com

In Australia, contact:
Hal Leonard Australia Pty. Ltd.
4 Lentara Court
Cheltenham, Victoria, 3192 Australia
Email: info@halleonard.com.au

Contents

10 Ac-cent-tchu-ate the Positive

16 Autumn Leaves

18 A Child Is Born

13 Choo Choo Ch'Boogie

20 Don't Worry, Be Happy

24 Fly Me to the Moon
    (In Other Words)

26 The Frim Fram Sauce

29 God Bless' the Child

32 How High the Moon

34 I Got Rhythm

39 I Loves You, Porgy

42 If I Didn't Have You

48 The Inch Worm

45 It Don't Mean a Thing
    (If It Ain't Got That Swing)

50 It's Only a Paper Moon

56 Java Jive

53 Lullaby of Birdland

60 Pennies from Heaven

65 Pick Yourself Up

70 Put On a Happy Face

73 Summertime

76 Sweet Georgia Brown

79 Take the "A" Train

86 A-Tisket A-Tasket

82 What a Wonderful World

Song Notes

Ac-cent-tchu-ate the Positive

According to the songwriting team of Harold Arlen and Johnny Mercer, the lyrics to this upbeat tune explain the key to happiness. Written in 1944 and first recorded by Mercer and The Pied Pipers, you'll want to accentuate the syncopation as well as the "positive" while sinking right into the jazzy harmony. Look at the chords in bars 5–6. Changing just one note changes the quality of the chord. First is **F major**: F-A-C. Change the C to C♯ and you have **F+** (**F augmented**): F-A-C♯. Change the C♯ to D and you have **F6**: F-A-D. This chord progression repeats several times throughout the song. Play with a little extra emphasis on those chord changes, and "Don't mess with Mister In-between!"

Autumn Leaves

Written in 1945 by Joseph Kosma with original French lyrics by Jacques Prevert and English lyrics by Johnny Mercer, this poignant melody is one of the most popular jazz standards of all time. A **standard** is a tune considered an important part of the jazz repertoire and widely known to both jazz musicians and listeners. "Autumn Leaves" is a standard both as a song and as an instrumental solo. A good place to start learning this simplified arrangement is with the opening four bars. A typical chord progression: Am7-D7-Gmaj7-Cmaj7-F♯m7♭5-B7-Em is repeated throughout. The number 7 in each of these chords represents the seventh note in the scale. For example, Am7 is played A-C-E-G (G is the seventh note of the A minor scale). Notice the left-hand part has a bit of a "falling" pattern, moving down by a 4th or 5th, and starting in bar 9, "falling" down by 7ths.

A Child Is Born

This beautiful jazz waltz was written in 1969 as an instrumental solo by trumpeter Thad Jones. Lyrics were independently added by Alec Wilder after he heard a performance by the Thad Jones-Mel Lewis Orchestra. Both song and instrumental versions have been covered (performed) by many artists over the years. Scan through the music to look for patterns. For example, play the first two bars. Compare the next two bars—they are the same. Compare bars 5–6 and you'll notice there is just one slight change to the rhythm in the melody. Bars 7–8 complete the phrase. Now play through bars 9–16 looking for similarities and differences. Continue through the rest of the arrangement and enjoy its lilting character.

Choo Choo Ch'Boogie

❧

In the style of jump blues, this energetic tune was written in 1946 by Vaughn Horton, Denver Darling, and Milt Gabler. **Jump blues** is an up-tempo style featuring horns and usually performed by a small group. It preceded rhythm and blues, and later, rock and roll. You can imagine the sound of a train whistle in the introduction, no doubt played by the horn section, but the distinctive left-hand bass line gives this arrangement its signature "boogie" sound. Note the fingering given to the recurring left-hand part in the first two bars. Instead of stretching your left hand, you can simply cross finger two over thumb to reach the E♭. Swing the eighth notes in the right hand. There's much repetition here. Compare bars 5–8 with bars 9–12. Notice what happens to the melody when you shift from the F chord to the B♭ chord. Play with a full sound and lots of energy in bars 17–24. Bring the train back to the station when you take the 2nd ending to finish the song.

Don't Worry, Be Happy

❧

Winner of the 1989 GRAMMY® Song of the Year, this upbeat number by Bobby McFerrin was composed and performed entirely with overdubbed vocal parts and other sounds made by the human voice. We've arranged this *a cappella* vibe for piano, and you'll definitely want to sing along as you play! Note the (♩♩ = ♩♪) next to the tempo heading at the beginning of the song and "swing" the eighth notes throughout. Begin by learning the first eight bars of the left-hand part. This repeating pattern allows you to focus on the fun syncopation in the right hand. "Don't worry," with a little practice you'll "be happy" to play this arrangement!

Fly Me to the Moon
(In Other Words)

❧

Originally titled "In Other Words," this 1954 Bart Howard tune was first performed and recorded by vocalist Kaye Ballard. Covered by jazz and cabaret singers over the years and often referred to as "Fly Me to the Moon," the title was officially changed in 1963. The melody begins with a distinctive dotted quarter-note rhythm. Set a steady pulse before you begin and take care to hold the dotted quarter-notes the full value. Don't rush into the eighth notes. Sink into the 7th chords harmonizing this lyrical tune. **7th chords** include the 7th note of the scale. For example, Am7 is played: A-C-E-G, and Dm7 is played: D-F-A-C. This stretches left hand just a bit, so practice feeling the distance of the 7th as you learn the chords.

The Frim Fram Sauce

❧

The King Cole Trio made this jazz song famous in 1945. Written by Redd Evans and Joe Ricardel, it was also recorded by Ella Fitzgerald with Louis Armstrong, and Diana Krall. **Frim fram** is a reference to trickery or fraud, particularly regarding money, sometimes also referred to as "flim flam." The rich harmony of this tune is full of 7th (seventh note of the scale added) and 9th (ninth note of the scale added) chords. Study bars 2–9 to make note of those chords and the accidentals added. Compare bars 10–17 and you'll see that it's the same as the previous section. Look ahead to bars 19–26 for new material, and more accidentals. Bar 27 to the end of the song repeats the material in the first two sections with a fun, accented ending.

God Bless' the Child

❧

Written in 1941 by Billie Holiday and frequent collaborator Arthur Herzog Jr., this moving song, covered by jazz artists including Aretha Franklin and Tony Bennett, was honored with a Grammy Hall of Fame Award. Listen for the beautiful harmony created by the lush chord changes and accidentals in this arrangement. **Accidentals** are sharps and flats not occurring in the key signature. In bars 3–4 there's a B♮ moving to a B♭ in the bass clef, and in bar 6 there's the colorful clash of B♭ in right hand against B♮ in left hand. Another example is in bars 7–8 right hand, first an A♮, then A♭. As you play, lean into the accidentals to enjoy the rich harmony they create.

How High the Moon

❧

This beautiful jazz standard was recorded by Benny Goodman & His Orchestra featuring vocalist Helen Forrest in 1940, and has been performed by many jazz musicians including The Les Paul Trio, Stan Kenton, and Ella Fitzgerald, among others. The interval of a 4th gives this lyrical melody its shape, right from the very first pick-up notes. (**Pick-up notes** are notes that occur before the first full beat of music.) The steady quarter notes provide a framework for the ever-changing harmony, but don't play too slowly. Carefully placed syncopation gives the melody a little push, so really highlight those rhythms in the left hand, and when they appear in the right-hand melody, such as bars 10 and 12.

I Got Rhythm

❧

This iconic jazz standard written in 1930 is the signature song of brothers George and Ira Gershwin. With a distinctive syncopated melody and trademark rhythm changes it was an instant hit and became the foundation for jazz writing in other popular tunes. Play the opening section freely to set the stage for the energetic "I Got Rhythm" section beginning at bar 29. Notice how the bass note in left hand alternates between A and D, even as the chords change above those notes. Set a strong pulse to determine where those syncopated changes occur, and play slowly at first, until you're comfortable moving from chord to chord.

I Loves You, Porgy

This poignant ballad is from the 1935 opera *Porgy and Bess* by George and Ira Gershwin and later made popular by jazz singer Nina Simone in 1958 on her album *Little Girl Blue*. Choose a slow tempo and play with as much *legato* as possible. Notice that the melody of the opening eight bars is composed almost entirely with intervals of a 3rd. The bass line anchors the melody, so be sure to hold the whole notes (as in bar 2) with finger 5 while you play the other left-hand notes in the measure. At bar 10 the tempo picks up just a bit, and with some added chromaticism, so does the drama. Carefully note the accidentals and don't shy away from emphasizing the colorful harmonies here. The last section is very similar to the first eight bars. Let the tempo slow just a bit as you bring this arrangement to a close.

If I Didn't Have You

This feel-good Randy Newman song was written for the 2001 Disney Pixar animated film *Monsters, Inc.* It won that year's Academy Award for Best Original Song. Sung by two of the film's main characters, Sully and Mike, this jazzy number needs a steady pulse and a playful vibe. The left-hand part remains simple throughout, giving you the opportunity to concentrate on the right-hand syncopation as you convey the story told by two good friends.

The Inch Worm

Written by Frank Loesser and originally performed by Danny Kaye in the 1952 film *Hans Christian Anderson*, this simple melody contains mostly 5ths and 6ths. Beginning with the four-bar introduction, you'll find a rising 6th (C to A) in the first bar, and a falling 5th (C to F) in the second bar. Read through the right-hand part to find the 5ths and 6ths, and you will have learned the song! Keep the left-hand accompaniment gentle, with a slight emphasis on each downbeat in phrases like bars 5–8 for a waltz-like feel. This song may be familiar to you, as it's appeared in many television shows and films, and performed by many artists, including David Bowie, Lisa Loeb, Paul McCartney, Anne Murray, and as an instrumental arrangement by the John Coltrane Quartet.

It Don't Mean a Thing
(If It Ain't Got That Swing)

This legendary tune was written in 1931 by Duke Ellington with lyrics by Irving Mills. First recorded in 1932, the Ellington band recorded this song numerous times, and the song has been performed widely by jazz greats such as Louis Armstrong, Tony Bennett, Ella Fitzgerald, Lionel Hampton, and the Modern Jazz Quartet, just to name a few. Enjoy the shifting rhythms throughout this catchy tune. Note the straight quarter notes in the first six bars, and contrast those with the syncopated eighth notes in bars 9–11. Really swing those rhythms and lean into the accented tied notes.

It's Only a Paper Moon

꧁

Originally written in 1933 by Harold Arlen with lyrics by Yip Harburg and Billy Rose, this song rose to fame during the last years of World War II with hit recordings by Nat King Cole, Ella Fitzgerald, and Benny Goodman, and has continued to be performed and recorded by various jazz artists since then. The syncopated melody begins not on the downbeat, but on the "and" of beat one. As you begin to learn this tune, be sure you've set a strong pulse so you know just where your downbeat is. This rhythm is repeated throughout. Skip ahead to the last bar for a lush and trademark jazz progression. Note the accidentals needed to play $A\flat$ $\frac{6}{9}$ ($A\flat$ chord with the 6th and 9th notes of the scale added) and then just move each note down a half-step to play the **G** $\frac{6}{9}$ chord.

Java Jive

꧁

Jive is a lively style of dance performed to swing music. This 1940 hit by Ben Oakland and Milton Drake is most well-known as recorded by The Ink Spots. There are accidentals and syncopation in the left-hand part, as well as a bit of a "walking" bass in bars 8, 12, and similar. Notice that all the left-hand notes span an octave, C to C for the first 12 bars, and shift in bars 14-17. The right-hand melody moves around a bit more. You'll want to "swing" the eighths throughout for a bouncy, jive feel. Once you feel comfortable playing each part, play hands together at a slow tempo, increasing your speed as you gain confidence. And maybe enjoy a cup of java too!

Lullaby of Birdland

꧁

George Shearing wrote this love song in 1952 for the famous New York City jazz club, **Birdland**. The composer begins in the key of E minor, but with the addition of G♯ in bar 19 you'll be playing in E major for the next eight bars before returning to E minor in bar 27. Play the swing eighths with a relaxed feel and a little extra stress on the syncopation created by eighth notes tied to half notes. Don't rush! Enjoy the changes and the rich chromatic harmony.

Pennies from Heaven

꧁

This Grammy Hall of Fame song was written in 1936 by Arthur Johnston and Johnny Burke. It was first recorded by Bing Crosby and also recorded by many jazz greats including Billie Holiday, Doris Day, Tony Bennett, and Dinah Washington. Play a bit freely with the tempo marked "moderately slow" to take extra time with both lyrics and the lovely chromatic harmony. Look for 7th chords (chords with the 7th note of the scale added, as in bars 4 and 6). Bar 22 uses a chord labeled G+ which means G augmented. **Augmented** chords are major chords with the 5th note of the scale raised a half step. In this case, instead of G major: G-B-D, you'll play G+: G-B-D♯.

Pick Yourself Up

———— ❧ ————

Covered by many artists through the decades, "Pick Yourself Up" was written by Jerome Kern and Dorothy Fields for the 1936 film *Swing Time*. This upbeat tune includes several key signature changes. Beginning in D major, at bar 19 we've moved to F major, changing again in bar 31, this time to G major. However, bar 39 finds us with a C major key signature and it's back to F major in bar 47 to the end. Keep things moving by always looking a bit ahead. Stay on your toes and remember: accidentals alter the note for the entire measure.

Put On a Happy Face

———— ❧ ————

Written for the 1960 Broadway musical *Bye Bye Birdie*, this bouncy tune is also known from the Oscar Peterson Trio's live album *Put On a Happy Face*. Listen to each of these renditions before you learn this arrangement. Can you play with characteristics of both? Really emphasize the eighth-note syncopation and lean into the 7th chords. Try a bit of improvisation yourself. Working with the first 16 bars, use the chord changes given and let the melody be a guide. Add passing notes and fill in where you can—just don't forget to put on your happy face!

Summertime

———— ❧ ————

George and Ira Gershwin, and DuBose and Dorothy Heyward wrote this soulful jazz standard for the 1935 opera *Porgy and Bess*, first performed by Abbie Mitchell. Notice the slow-moving blues harmony with changes on each half note. Really sink into those chords and set a solid tempo that allows melody and lyrics to float above the harmony. Most of the time Gershwin uses just five notes of the A minor scale for his melody: A-B-C-D-E. Don't rush the rests. Breathe as you begin each phrase with care.

Sweet Georgia Brown

———— ❧ ————

Although written and recorded in 1925 by Ben Bernie and his Hotel Roosevelt Orchestra (lyrics by Maceo Pinkard) the most popular version of this jaunty tune was recorded in 1949 by Brother Bones, and it's his version that's become the Harlem Globetrotters' theme music. Look at the right-hand melody. It's a bit angular, meaning the intervals move both up and down. Spend time naming the intervals as you learn the right-hand part. For example, beginning in bars 5–6 you have notes moving up by 2nds, down by 3rd, up by 5th, down by 3rd, up by 4th and so on. Compare bars 5–6 with bars 9–10. You'll note the same intervals, but this time the F♯s are now F♮. The interplay between major and minor gives this tune a twist. The left-hand part is very straightforward; think about giving the walking bass between the chord changes just a bit of emphasis.

Take the "A" Train

This iconic signature tune of the Duke Ellington Orchestra was first recorded in 1941. The title refers to the then-new "A" subway line that ran through New York City. You'll want to become very familiar with the spiffy moving bass line in left hand. The rhythm can seem simple, mostly moving in quarter notes, but the added **accidentals** (sharps and flats) really add a lot of color and forward motion. The left-hand part repeats every eight bars, so once you learn bars 3–10 you're ready to leave the station! There's a tricky bit for right hand in bars 8–10. Follow the fingering given and play those bars slowly at first. And don't forget to swing the eighths! The right-hand part repeats just like the left hand, so working on this section will have you playing the whole arrangement in no time.

A-Tisket A-Tasket

The amazing jazz singer Ella Fitzgerald used the nursery rhyme "A-Tisket A-Tasket" to create a breakthrough hit with the Chick Webb Orchestra in 1938. Despite some syncopation you'll recognize the familiar melody, so choose an upbeat tempo and swing the eighth notes. The left-hand part stays within an octave range; once you find your starting notes the left hand can settle in. The middle section melody (bars 17–24) contrasts with the traditional tune and includes more syncopation and new accidentals. Work through this section on its own and then play the whole song.

What a Wonderful World

This lovely jazz ballad was recorded by Louis Armstrong in 1967, and first topped the charts in the UK before its reissue in 1988, when it was used in the hit film *Good Morning, Vietnam*. Written by George David Weiss and Bob Thiele, it remains a signature song associated with Armstrong and has since become a jazz standard in the U.S. Even with the slow tempo of this ballad you'll want to swing the eighth notes. There are two types of triplets in the melody: **eighth-note triplets** (three eighths equal one beat) and **quarter note triplets** (three quarter notes equal two beats). Setting a steady pulse throughout helps keep the structure of the melody intact. Even with a steady beat you can play with a bit of freedom and rubato, so sing along and use the lyrics to guide you. Left-hand accompaniment almost always spans an octave, so move your left-hand finger 5 down to each bass note, stretching up the octave with your thumb.

Ac-cent-tchu-ate the Positive

from the Motion Picture HERE COME THE WAVES

Lyric by JOHNNY MERCER
Music by HAROLD ARLEN

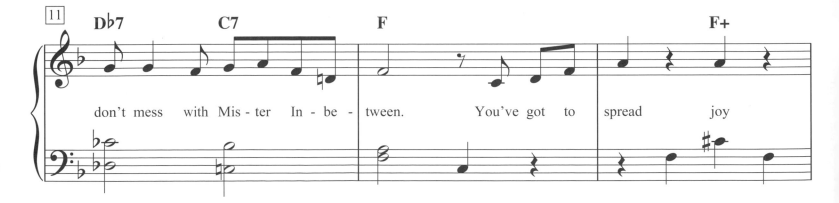

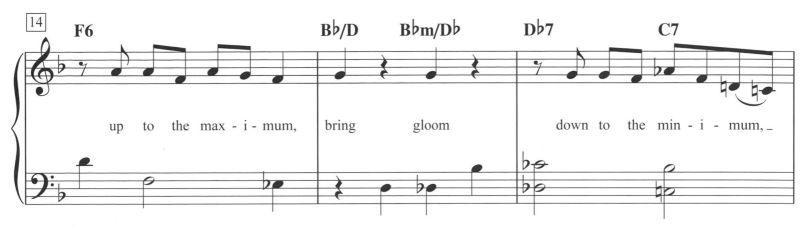

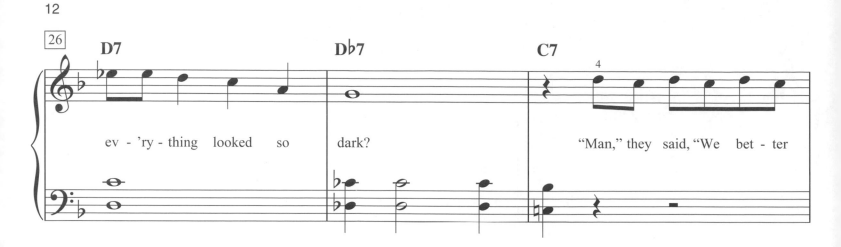

26 **D7**   **Db7**   **C7**

ev - 'ry - thing looked so dark?   "Man," they said, "We bet - ter

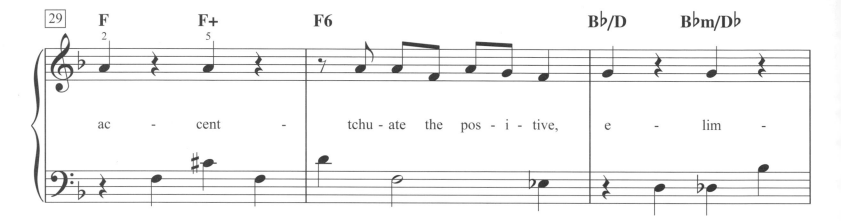

29 **F**   **F+**   **F6**   **Bb/D**   **Bbm/Db**

ac - cent - tchu - ate the pos - i - tive,   e - lim -

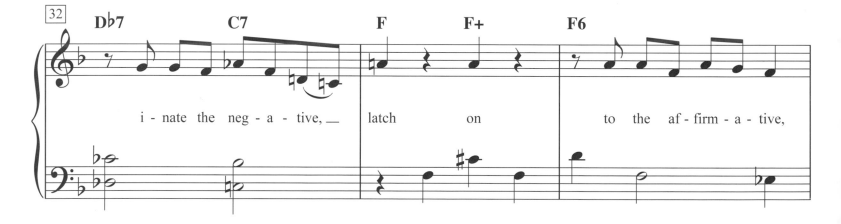

32 **Db7**   **C7**   **F**   **F+**   **F6**

i - nate the neg - a - tive, __ latch on to the af - firm - a - tive,

35 **Db7**   **C7**   **F**   **D7b9**   **Gm7**   **F**   **F(add9)**

don't mess with Mis - ter In - be - tween." No! Don't mess with Mis - ter In - be - tween.

Choo Choo Ch'Boogie

Words and Music by VAUGHN HORTON,
DENVER DARLING and MILTON GABLER

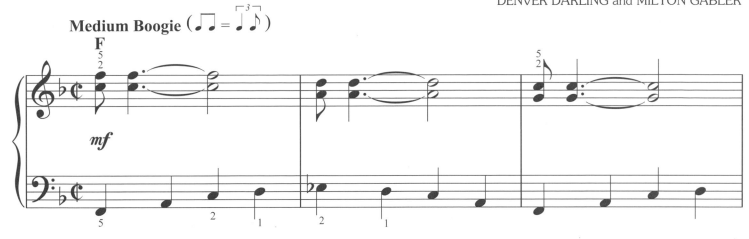

click - e - ty clack, ___ and hear the lone - some whis - tle, see the
top of the stack, ___ and read the sit - u - a - tion from the

smoke from the stack. ___ And pal a - round with dem - o - crat - ic
front to the back. ___ The on - ly job that's o - pen needs a

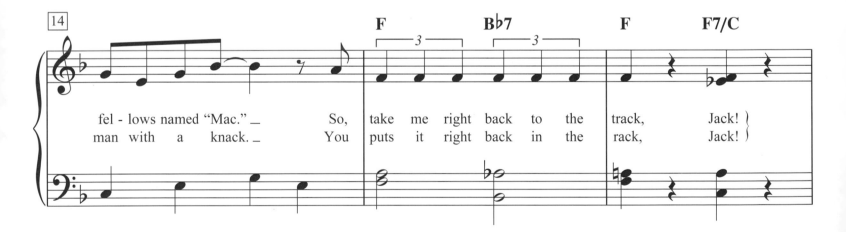

fel - lows named "Mac." __ So, take me right back to the track, Jack! }
man with a knack. __ You puts it right back in the rack, Jack! }

Choo choo _____ choo-choo - ch - boo - gie, woo - woo _____

boo - gie - woo - gie. Choo choo _____ choo-choo - ch - boo - gie,

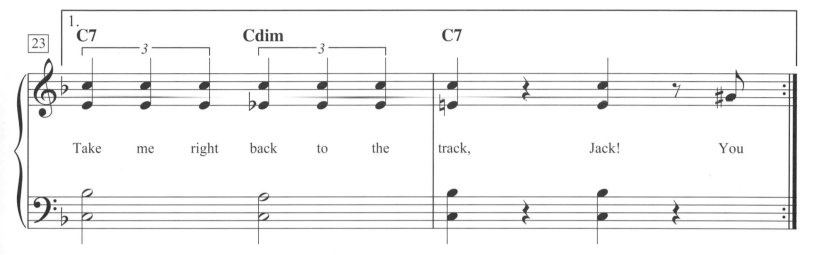

Take me right back to the track, Jack! You

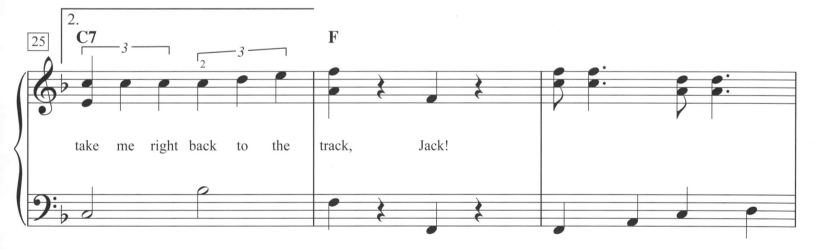

take me right back to the track, Jack!

Autumn Leaves

English lyric by JOHNNY MERCER
French lyric by JACQUES PREVERT
Music by JOSEPH KOSMA

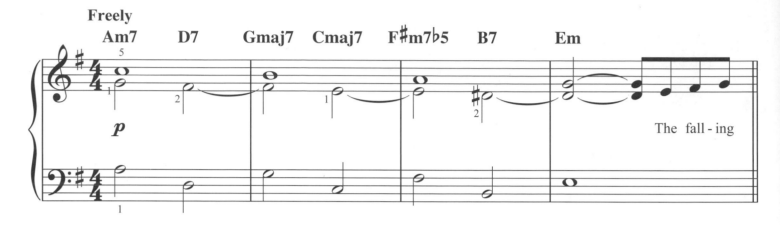

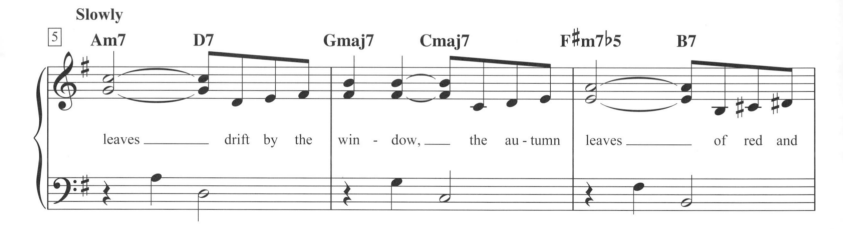

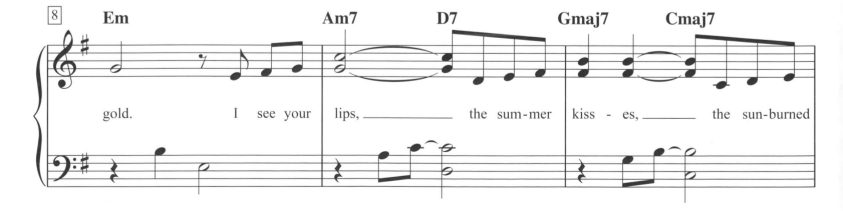

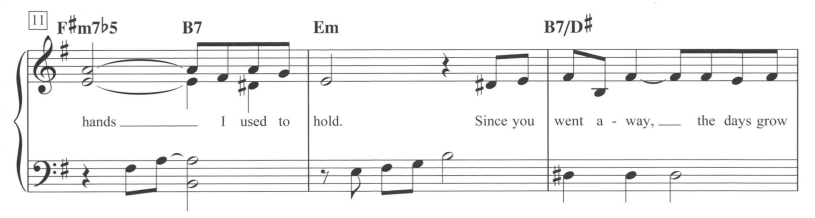

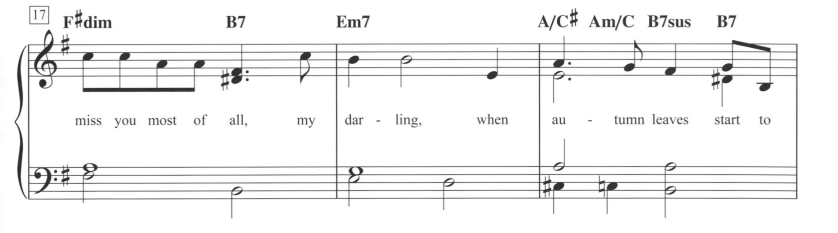

A Child Is Born

Music by THAD JONES
Lyrics by ALEC WILDER

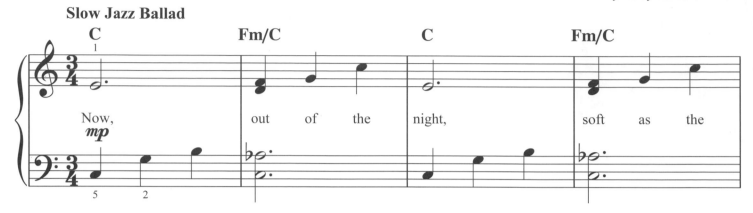

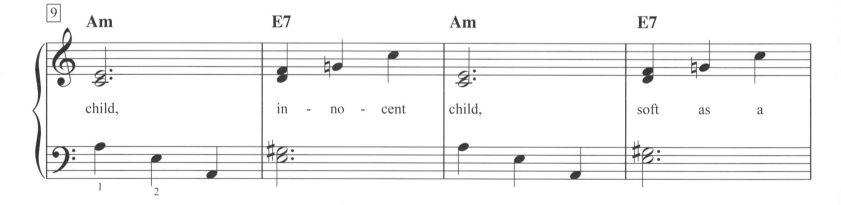

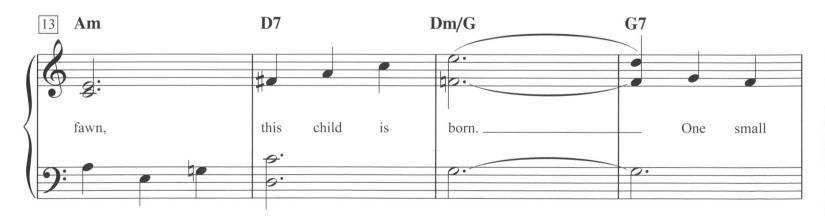

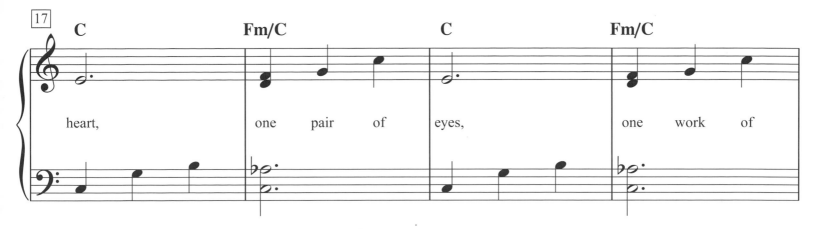

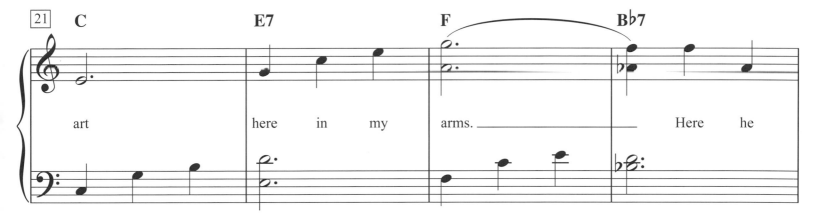

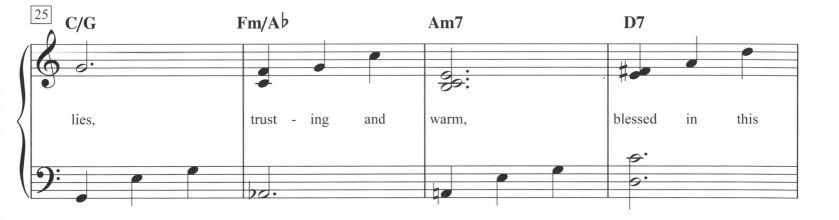

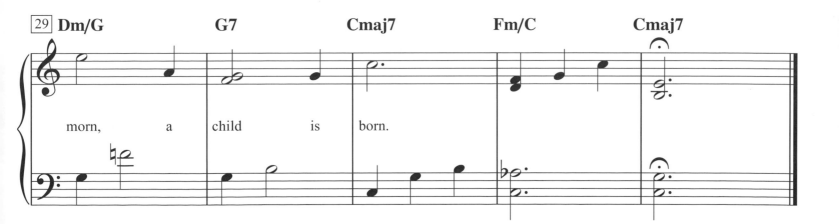

Don't Worry, Be Happy

Words and Music by
BOBBY McFERRIN

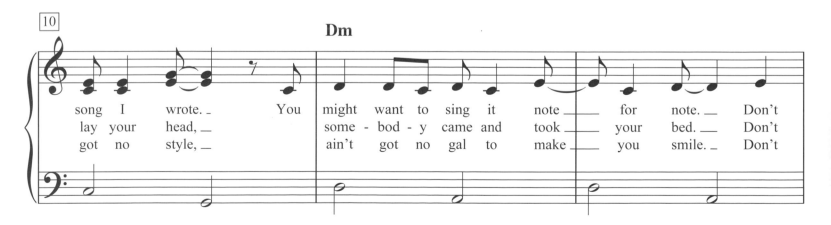

21

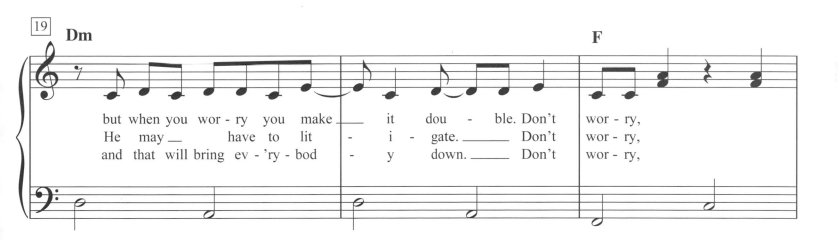

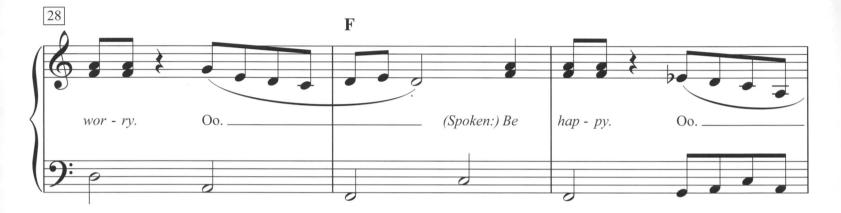

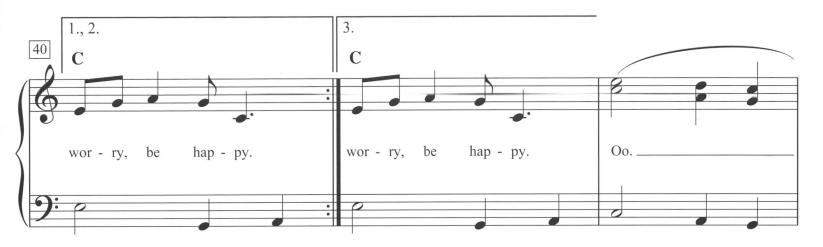

Fly Me to the Moon
(In Other Words)

Words and Music by
BART HOWARD

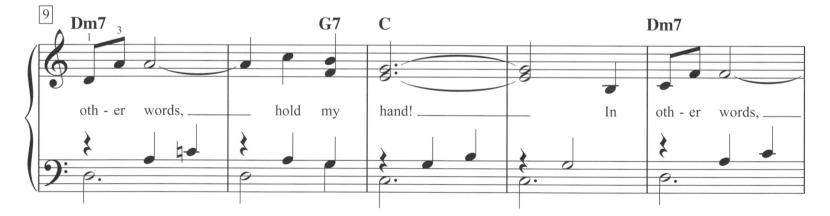

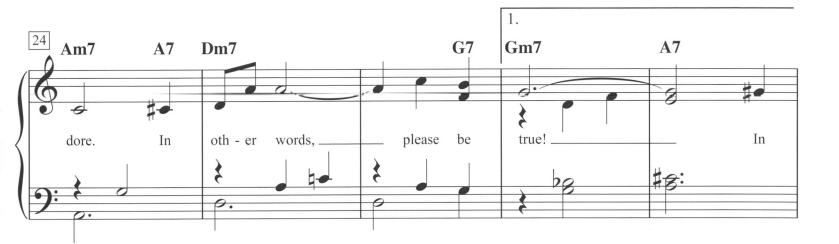

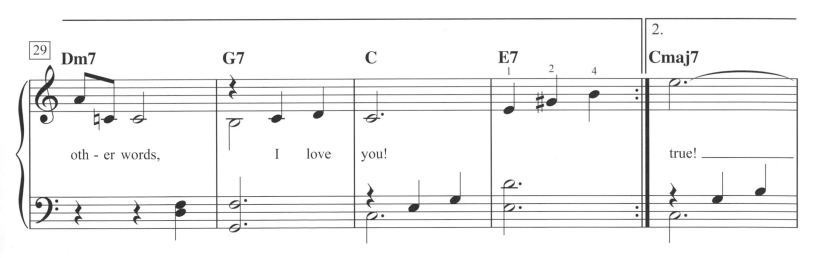

The Frim Fram Sauce

Words and Music by JOE RICARDEL
and REDD EVANS

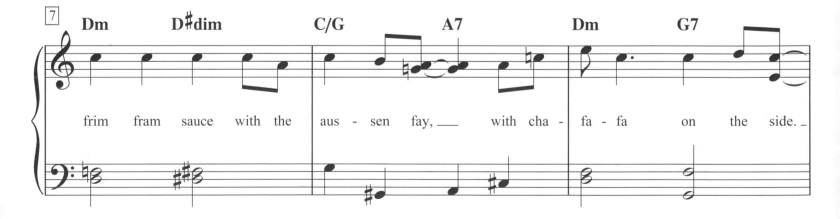

Five will get you ten, ___ I'm gon - na feed my - self right ___ to - night.

___ I don't want fish cakes and rye bread, you heard what I said.

Wait - er, please serve ___ mine fried. ___ I want the frim fram sauce with the

aus - sen fay ___ with cha - fa - fa on the side. ___

God Bless' the Child

Words and Music by ARTHUR HERZOG JR.
and BILLIE HOLIDAY

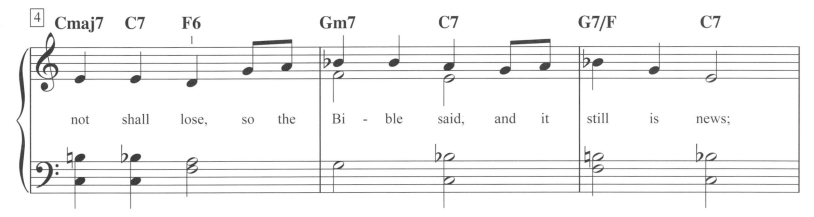

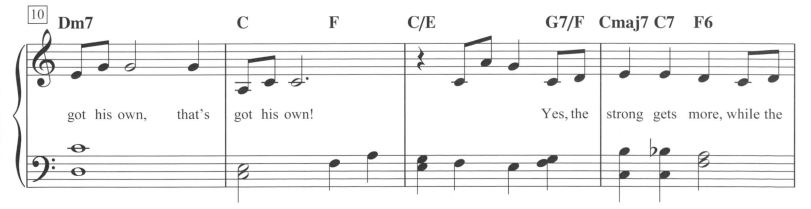

14 | Cmaj7 C7 F6 | Gm7 C7 | G7/F C7 | F

weak ones fade, emp - ty | pock - ets don't ev - er | make the grade; | Ma - ma may have,

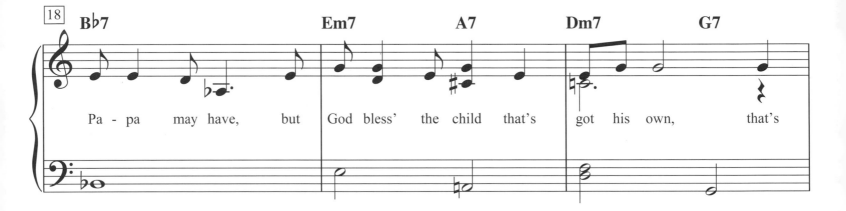

18 | Bb7 | Em7 A7 | Dm7 G7

Pa - pa may have, but | God bless' the child that's | got his own, that's

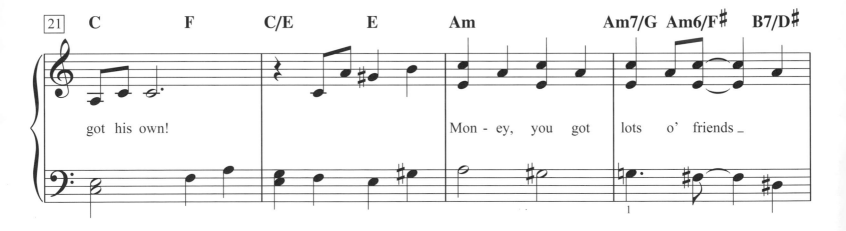

21 | C F | C/E E | Am | Am7/G Am6/F# B7/D#

got his own! | | Mon - ey, you got | lots o' friends

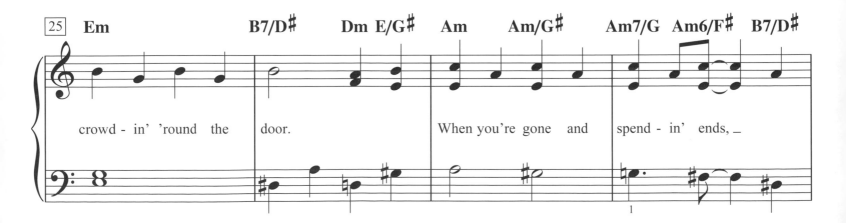

25 | Em B7/D# | Dm E/G# Am Am/G# | Am7/G Am6/F# B7/D#

crowd - in' 'round the | door. When you're gone and | spend - in' ends,

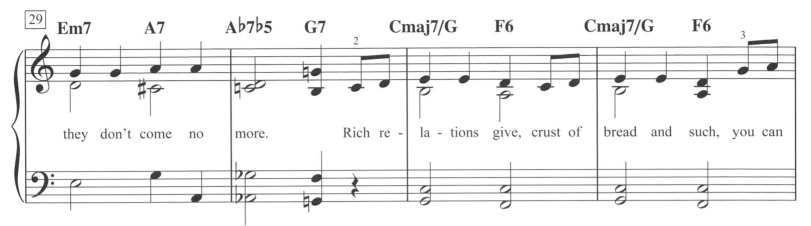

they don't come no more. Rich re - la - tions give, crust of bread and such, you can

help you - self, but don't take too much! Ma - ma may have, Pa - pa may have, but

God bless' the child that's got his own! That's got his own.

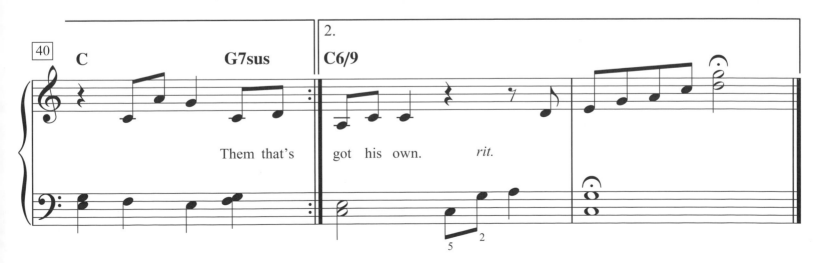

Them that's got his own. *rit.*

How High the Moon

from TWO FOR THE SHOW

Lyrics by NANCY HAMILTON
Music by MORGAN LEWIS

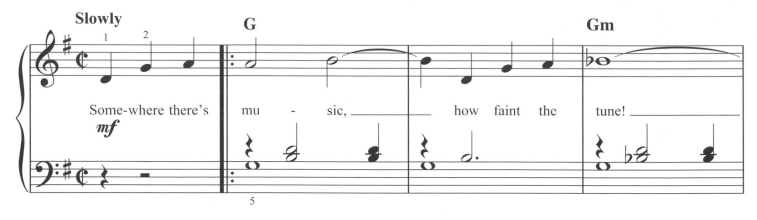

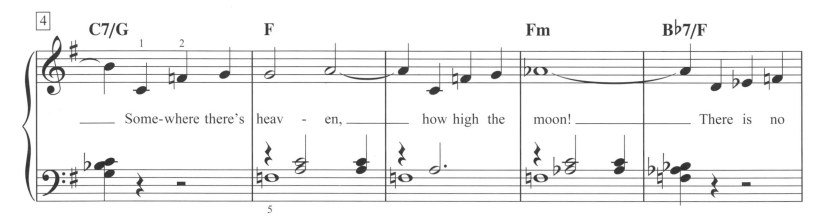

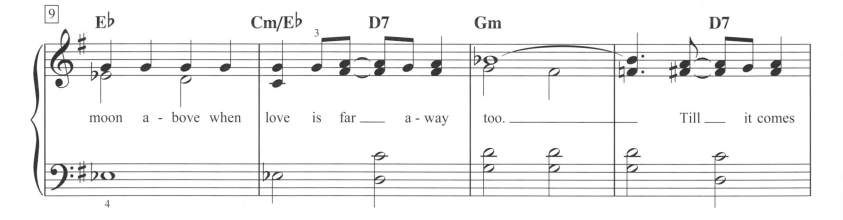

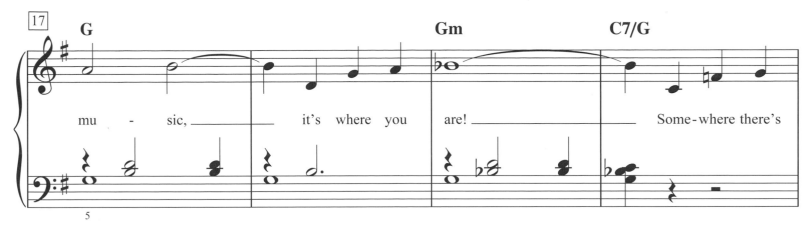

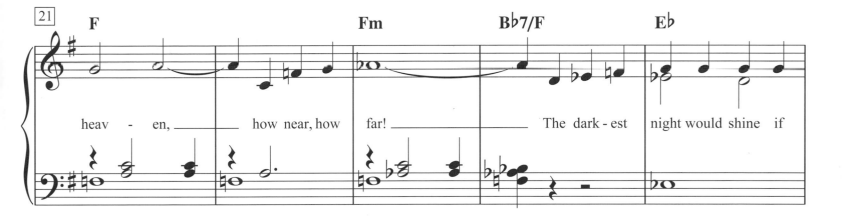

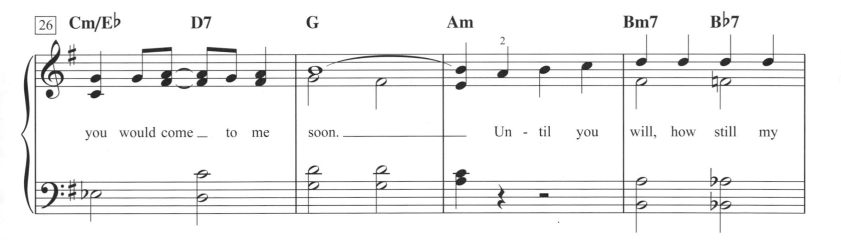

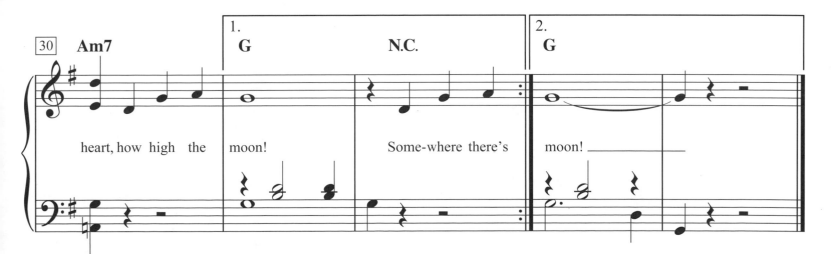

I Got Rhythm

from GIRL CRAZY

Music and Lyrics by GEORGE GERSHWIN
and IRA GERSHWIN

Moderately, somewhat rubato

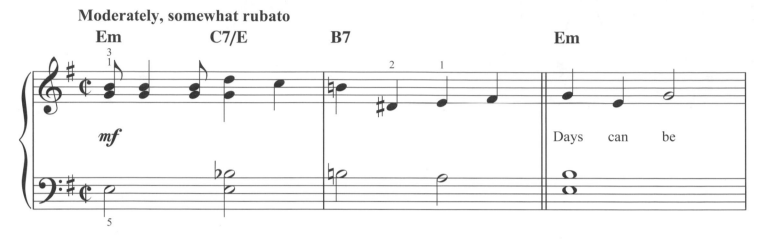

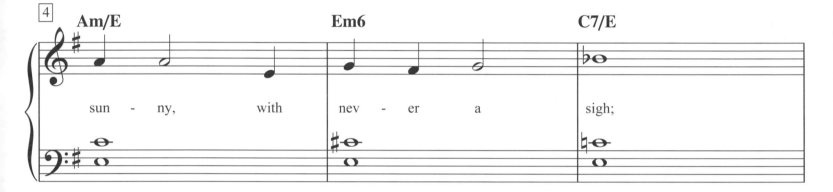

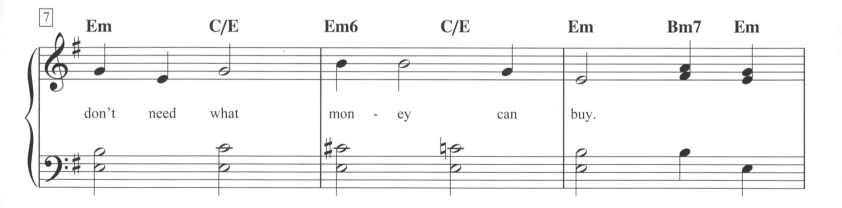

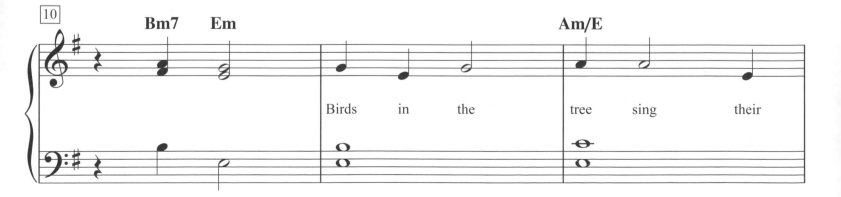

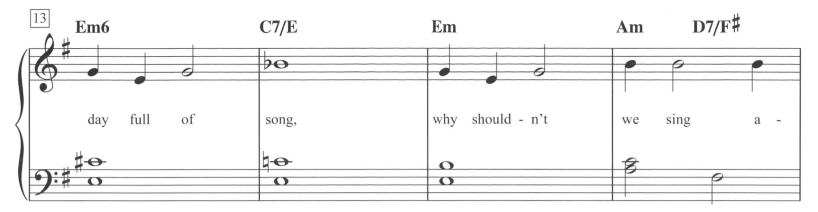

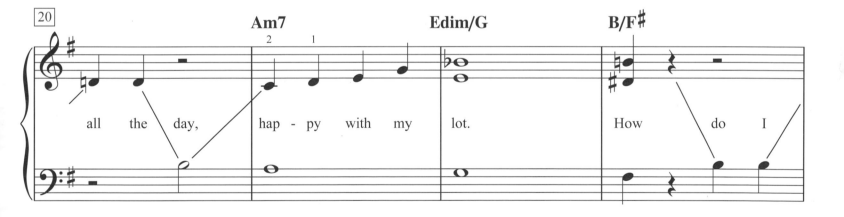

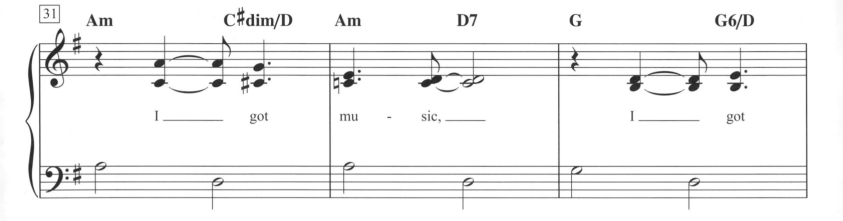

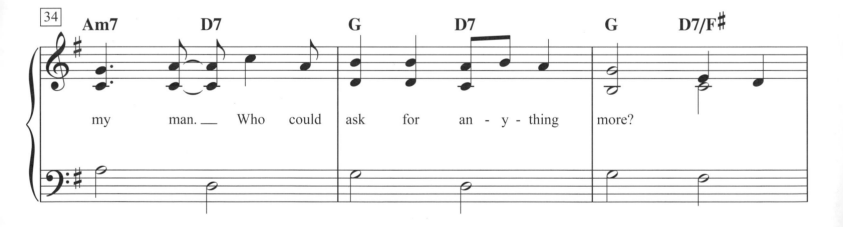

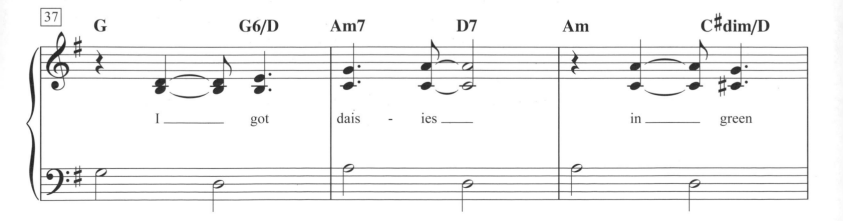

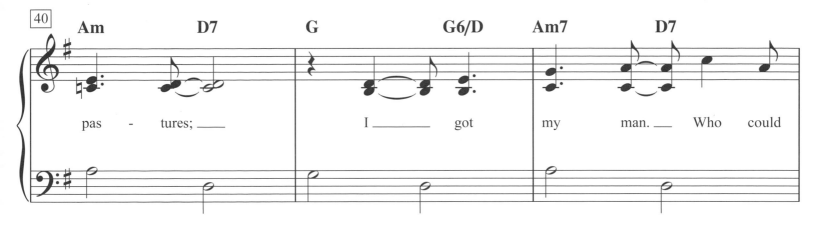

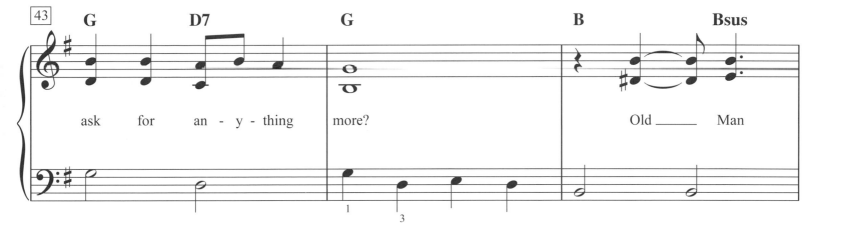

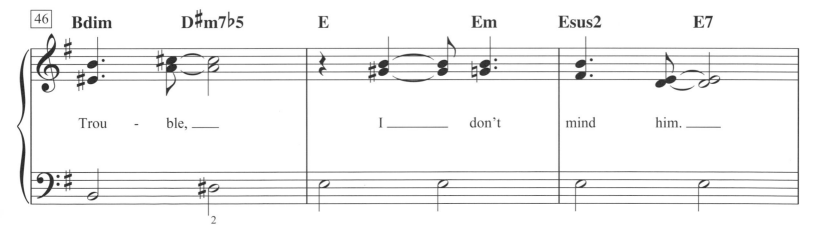

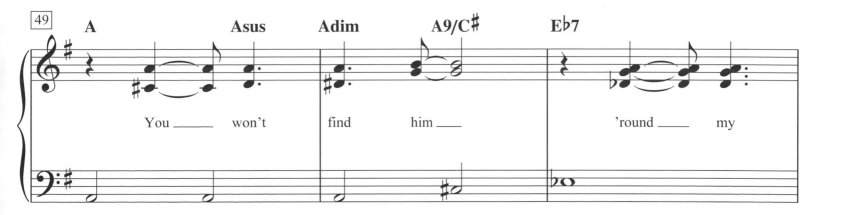

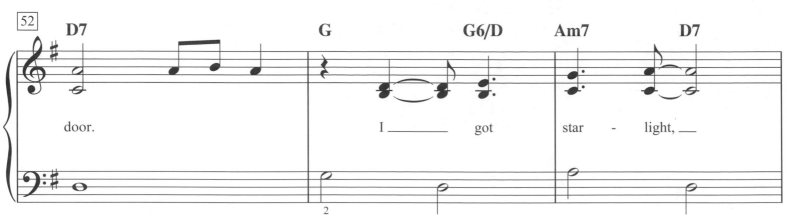

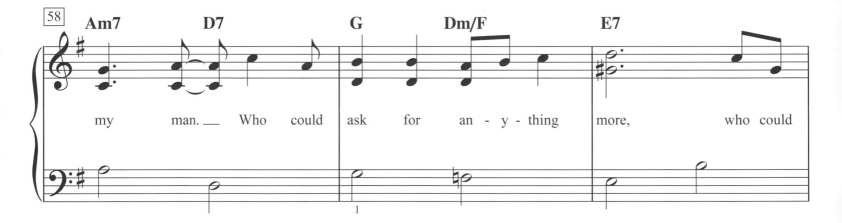

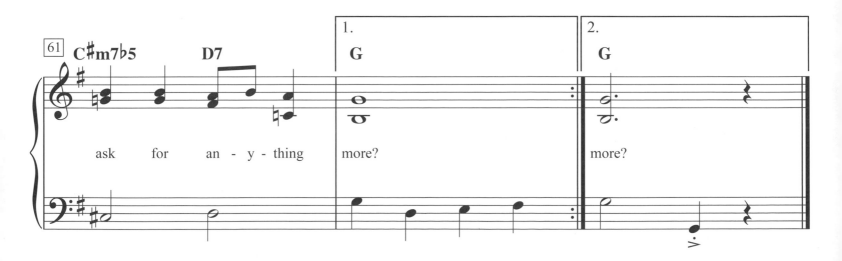

I Loves You, Porgy

from PORGY AND BESS®

Music and Lyrics by GEORGE GERSHWIN,
DuBOSE and DOROTHY HEYWARD and IRA GERSHWIN

Slowly, with feeling

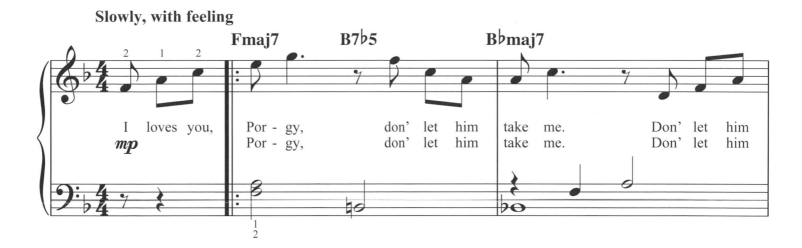

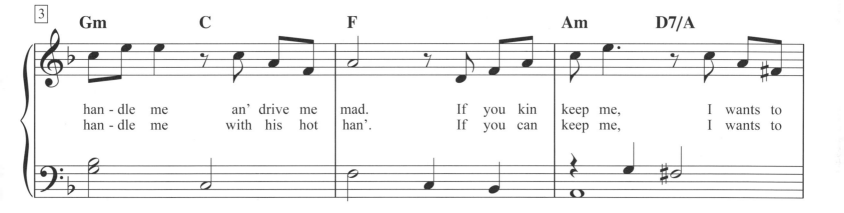

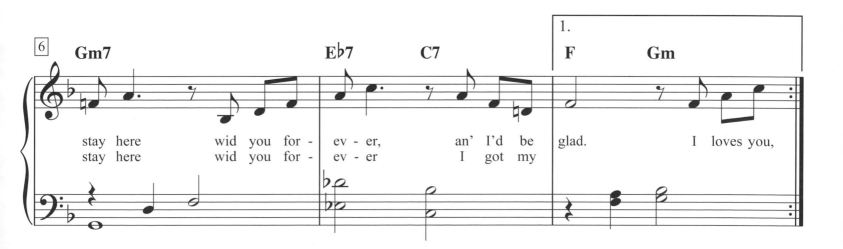

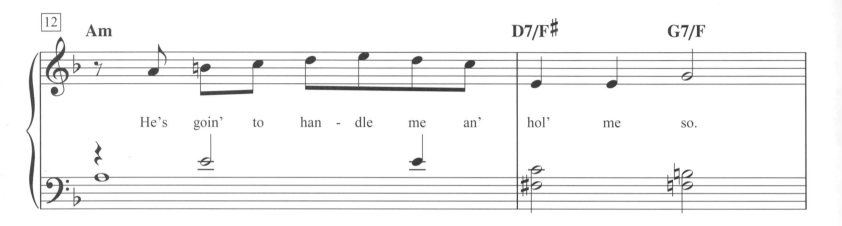

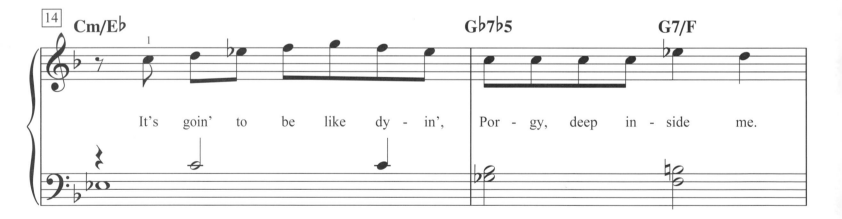

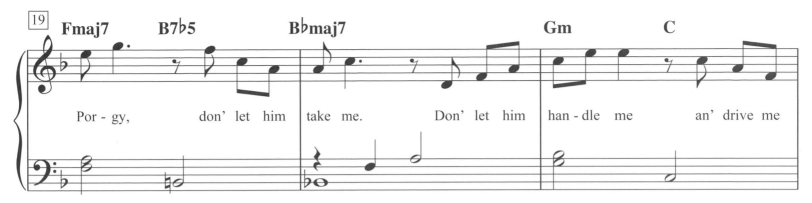

If I Didn't Have You

from MONSTERS, INC.

Music and Lyrics by
RANDY NEWMAN

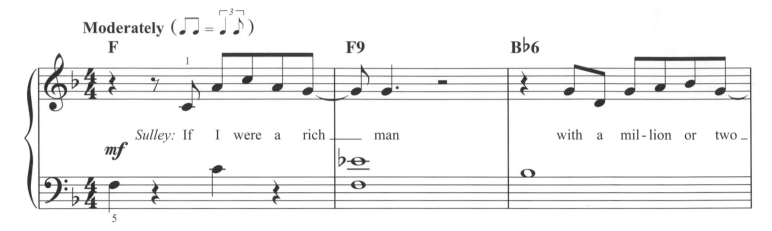

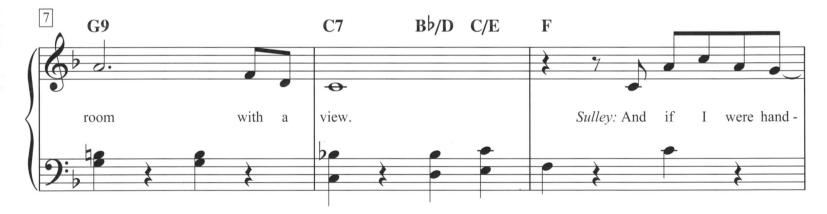

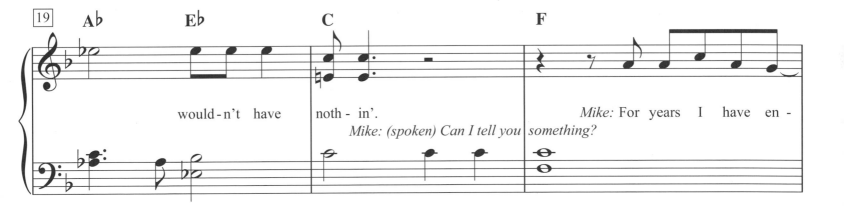

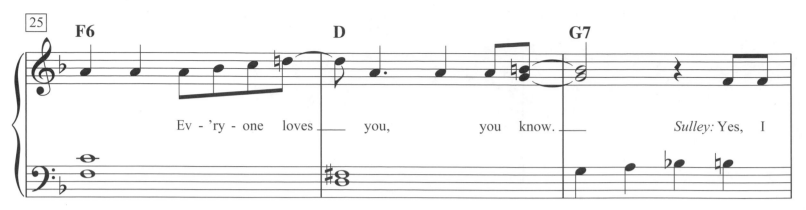

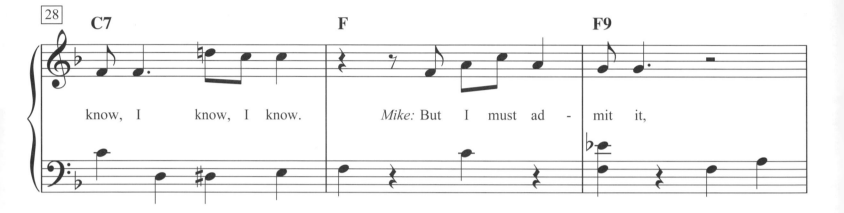

It Don't Mean a Thing
(If It Ain't Got That Swing)

Words and Music by DUKE ELLINGTON
and IRVING MILLS

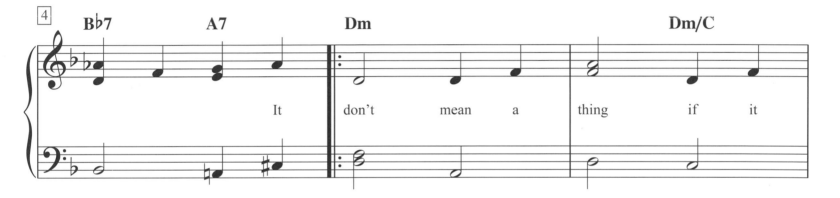

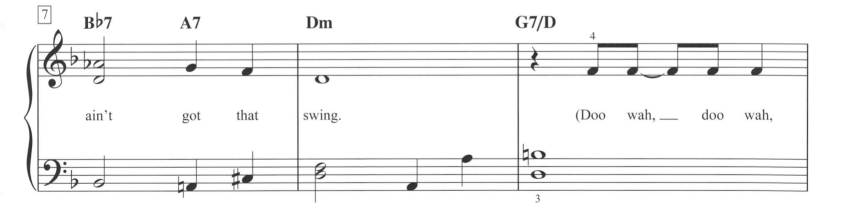

don't mean a thing, all you got to do is

sing. (Doo wah, __ doo wah, doo wah, doo wah, doo wah, __

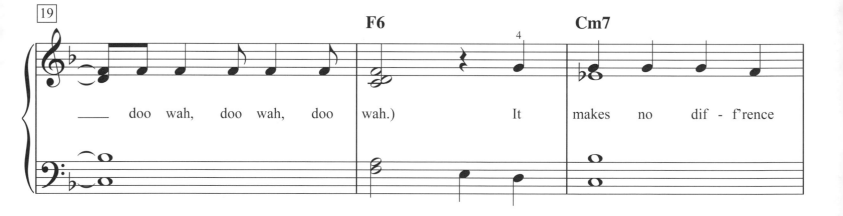

__ doo wah, doo wah, doo wah.) It makes no dif - f'rence

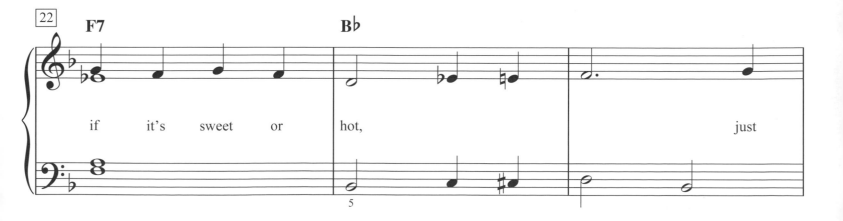

if it's sweet or hot, just

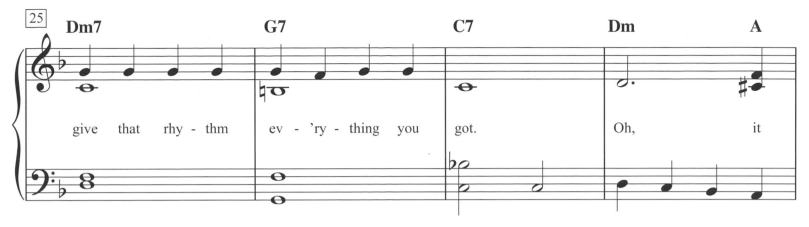

give that rhy - thm ev - 'ry - thing you got. Oh, it

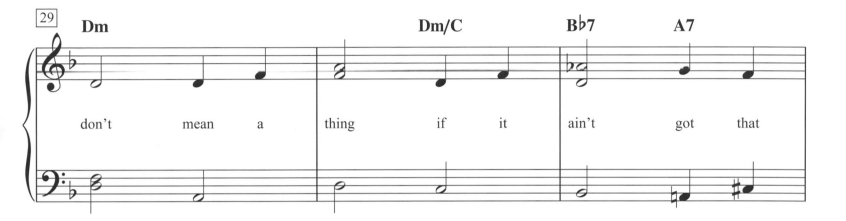

don't mean a thing if it ain't got that

swing. (Doo wah, __ doo wah, doo wah, doo wah, doo wah, __

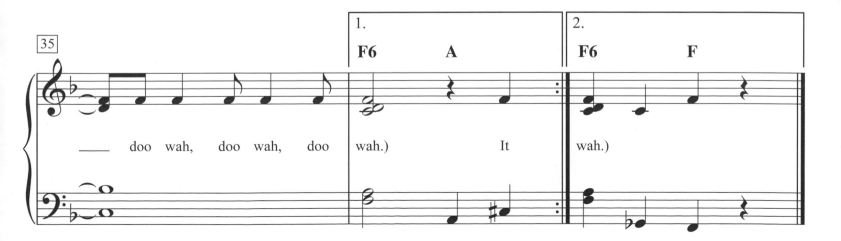

__ doo wah, doo wah, doo wah.) It wah.)

The Inch Worm

from the Motion Picture HANS CHRISTIAN ANDERSON

By FRANK LOESSER

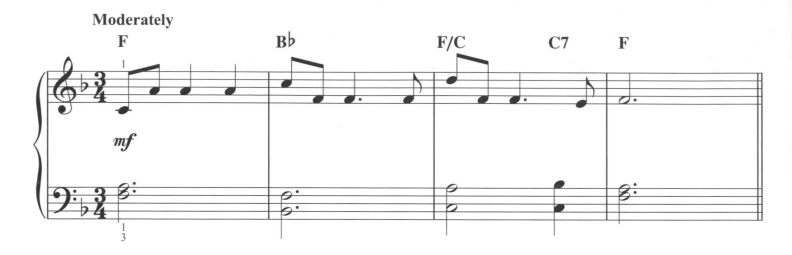

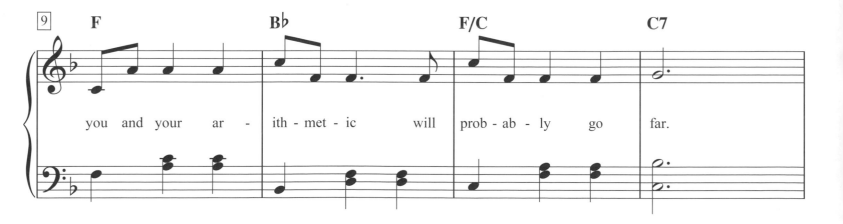

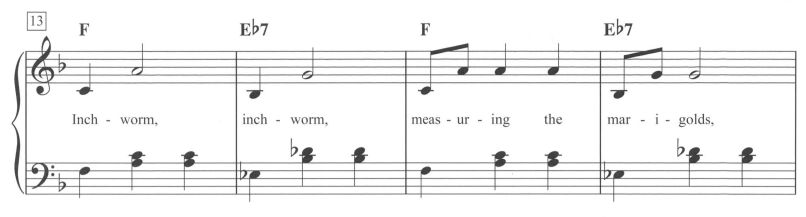

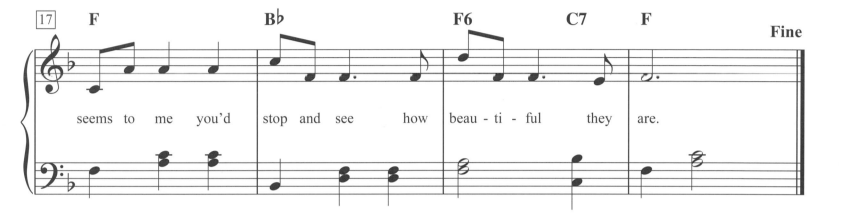

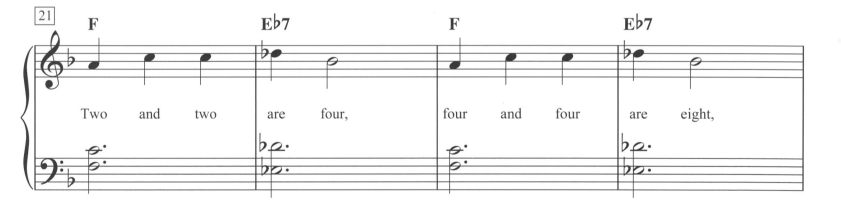

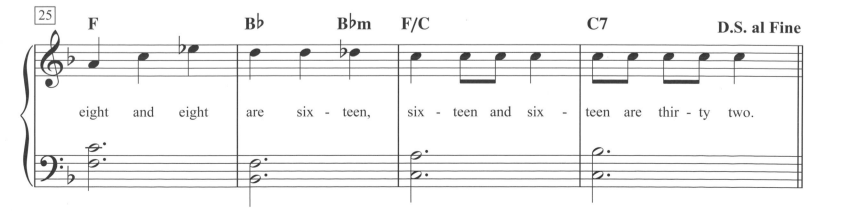

It's Only a Paper Moon

Lyric by BILLY ROSE and E.Y. "YIP" HARBURG
Music by HAROLD ARLEN

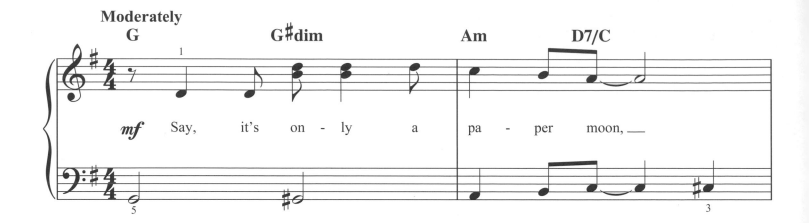

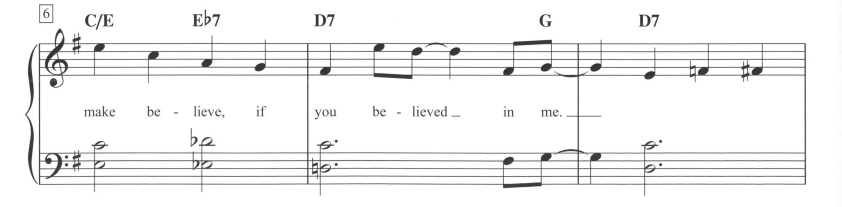

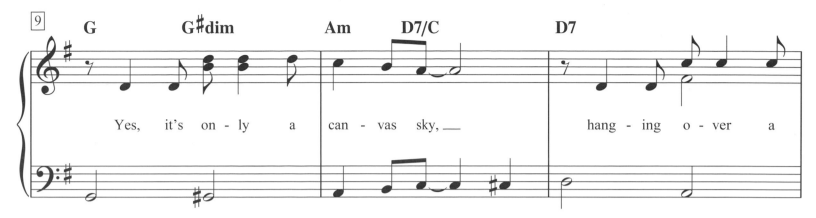

Yes, it's on - ly a can - vas sky, __ hang - ing o - ver a

mus - lin tree, __ but it would - n't be make be - lieve, if

you be - lieved __ in me. __ With - out your

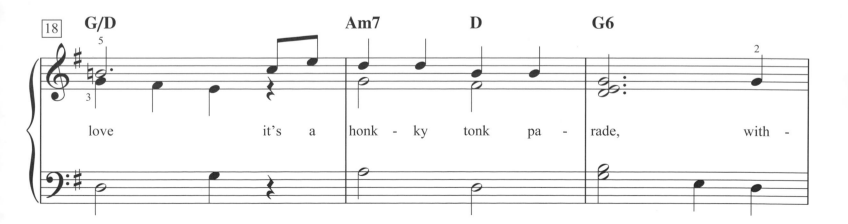

love it's a honk - y tonk pa - rade, with -

52

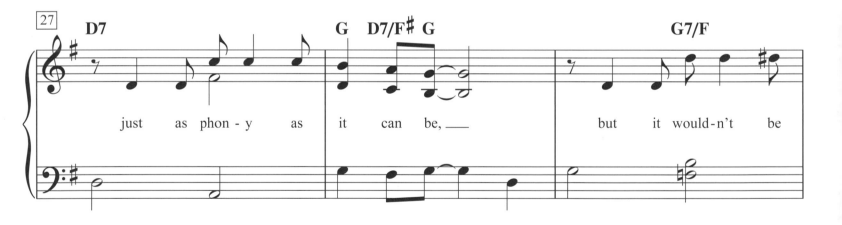

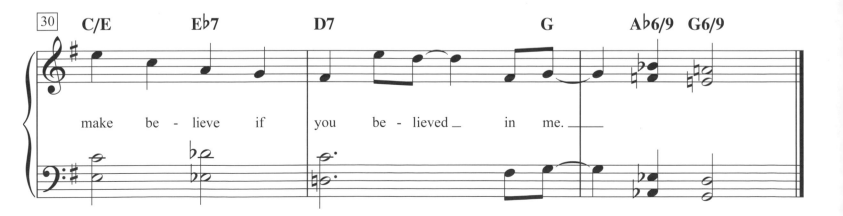

Lullaby of Birdland

Words by GEORGE DAVID WEISS
Music by GEORGE SHEARING

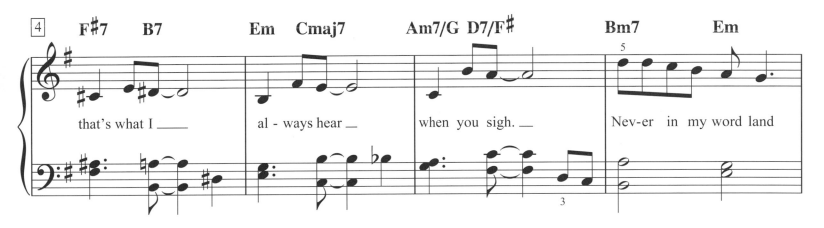

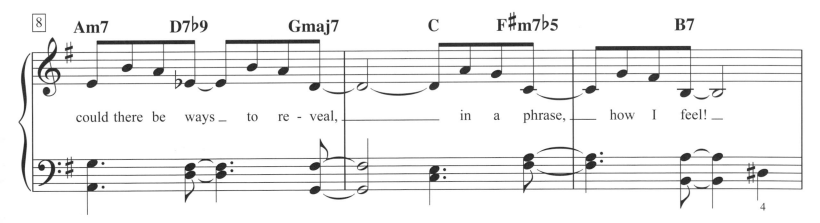

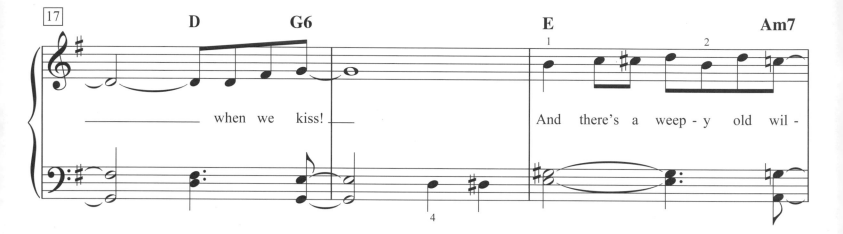

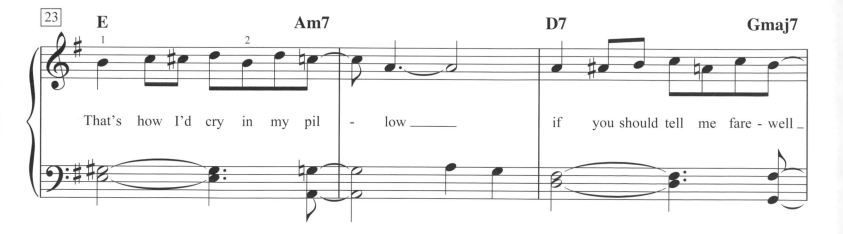

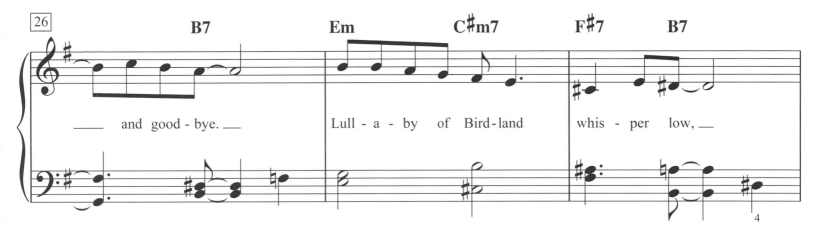

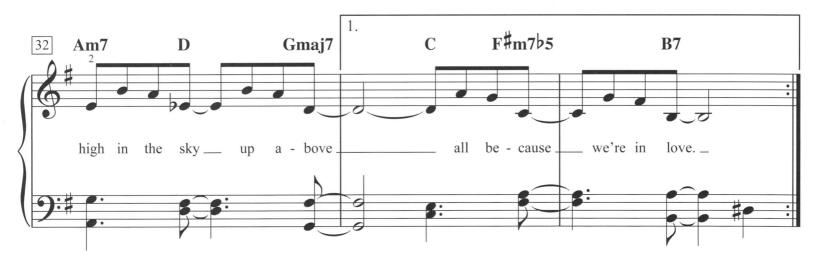

Java Jive

Words and Music by MILTON DRAKE
and BEN OAKLAND

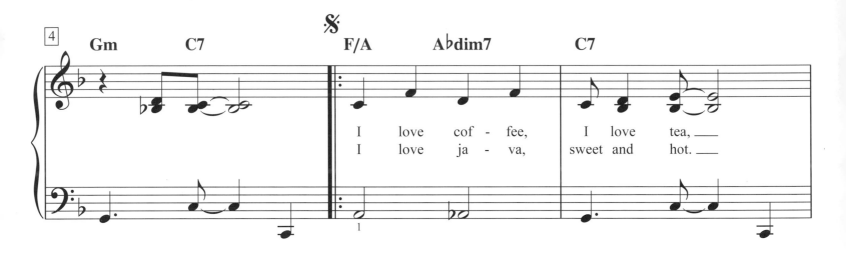

I love cof - fee, I love tea, ___
I love ja - va, sweet and hot. ___

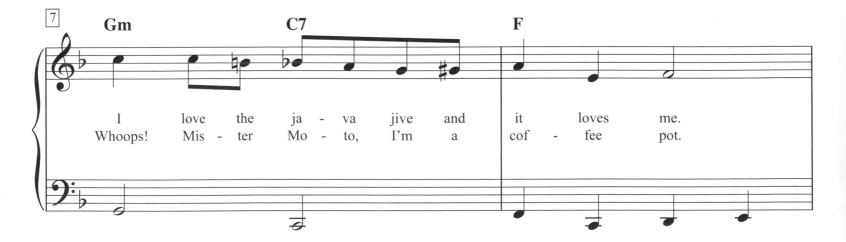

I love the ja - va jive and it loves me.
Whoops! Mis - ter Mo - to, I'm a cof - fee pot.

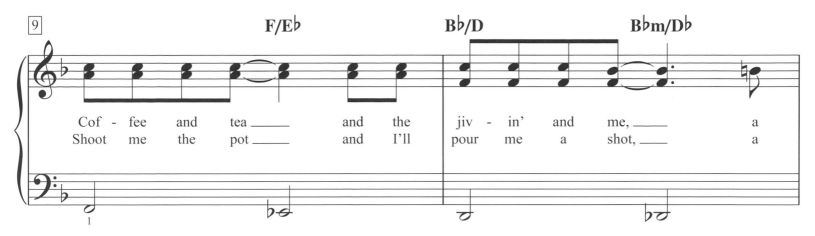

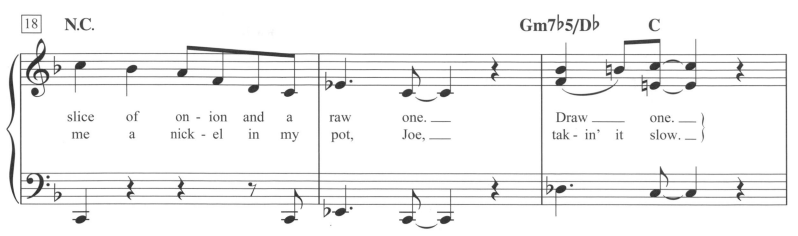

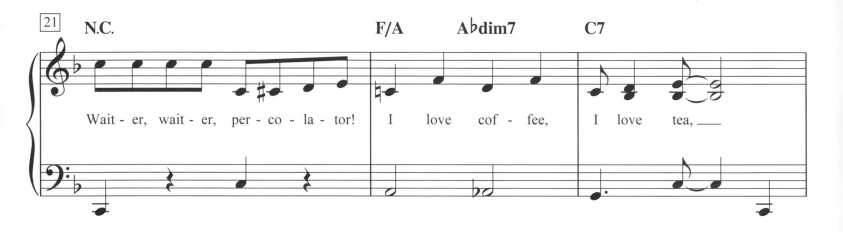

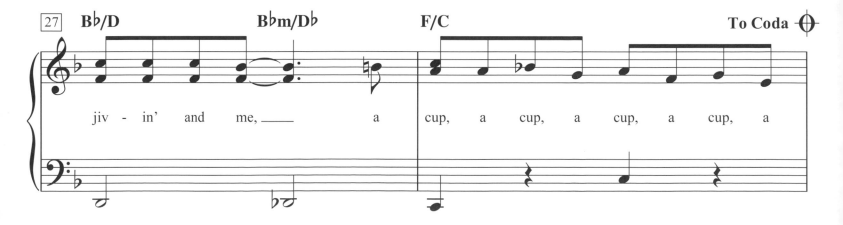

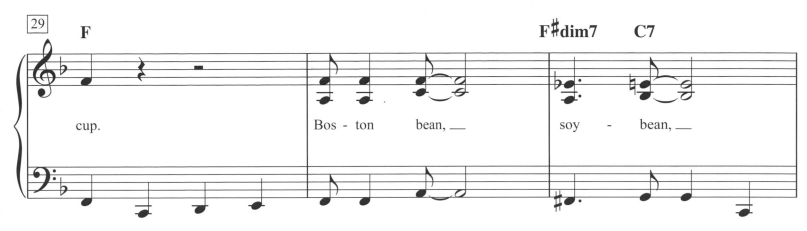

cup. Bos - ton bean, ___ soy - bean, ___

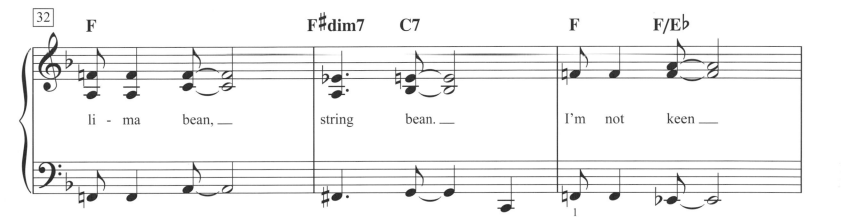

li - ma bean, ___ string bean. ___ I'm not keen ___

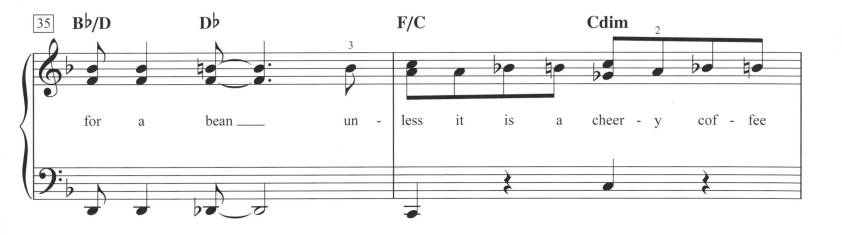

for a bean ___ un - less it is a cheer - y cof - fee

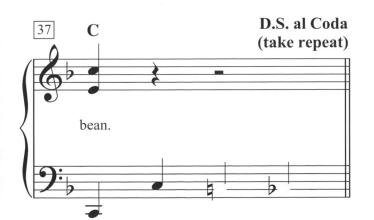

bean.

D.S. al Coda
(take repeat)

CODA

cup.

Pennies from Heaven

from PENNIES FROM HEAVEN

Words by JOHN BURKE
Music by ARTHUR JOHNSTON

Moderately slow

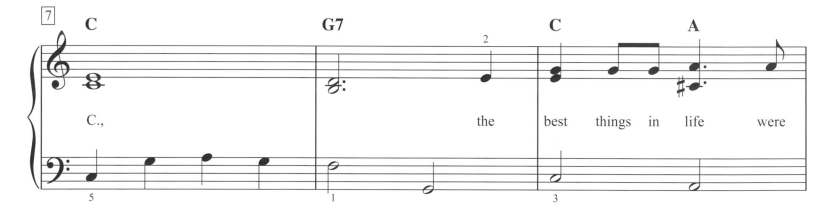

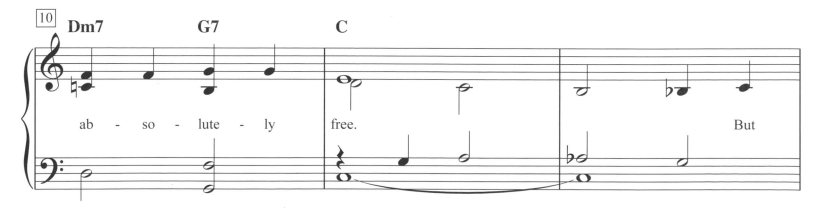

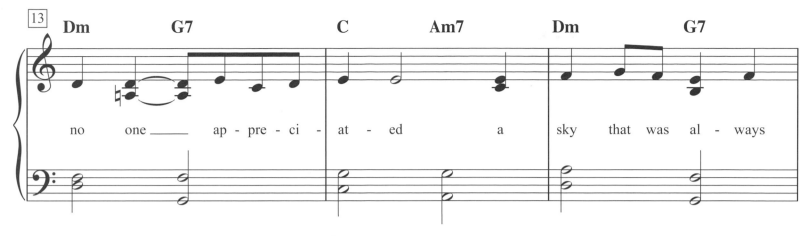

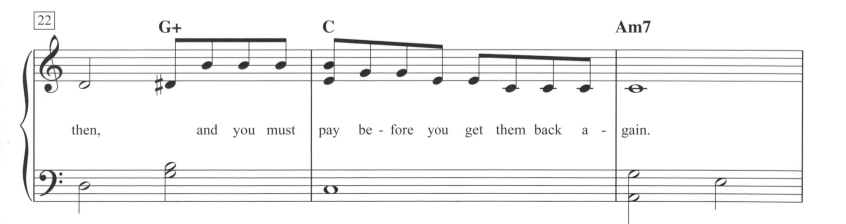

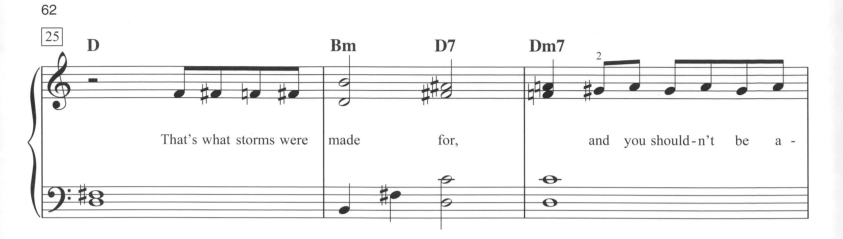

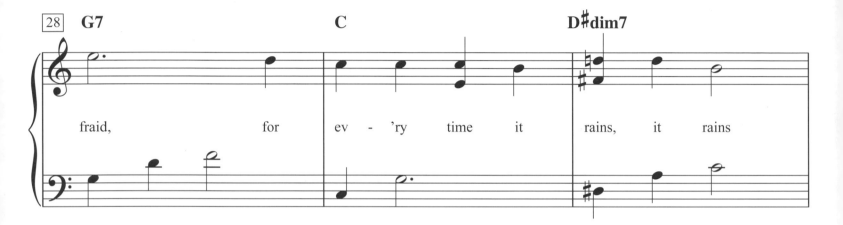

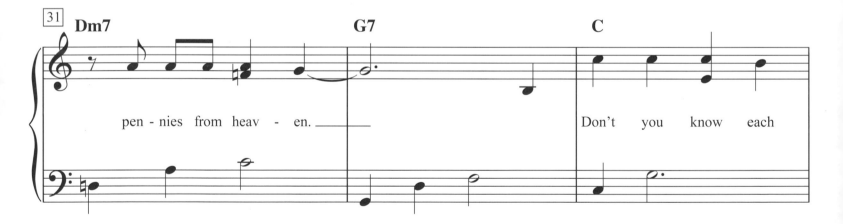

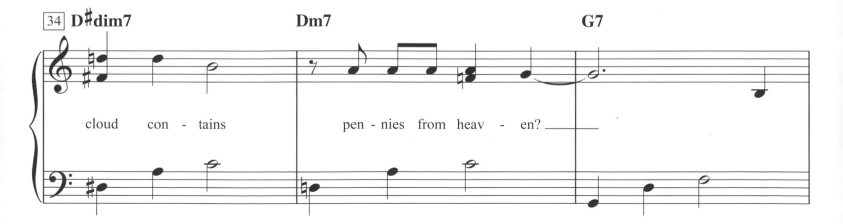

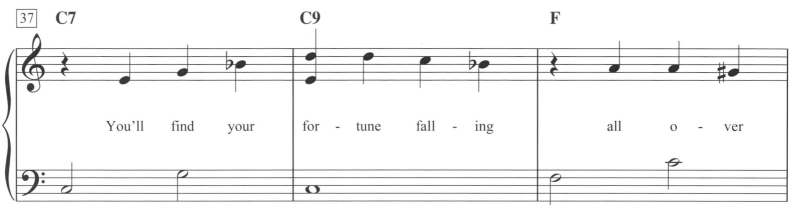

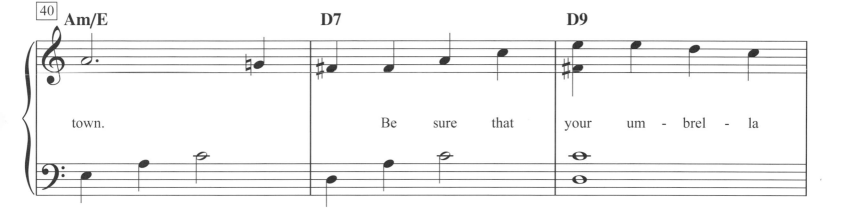

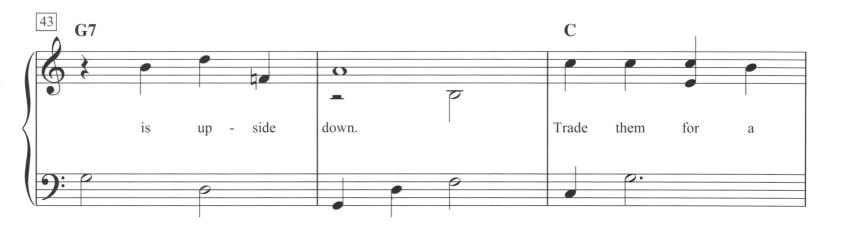

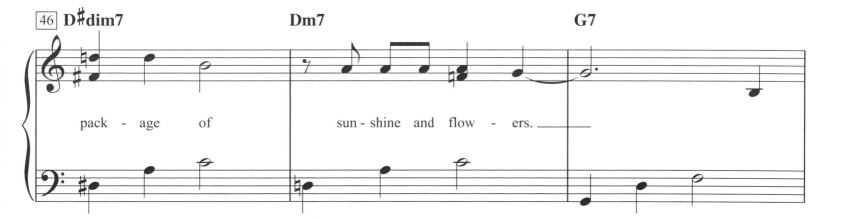

64

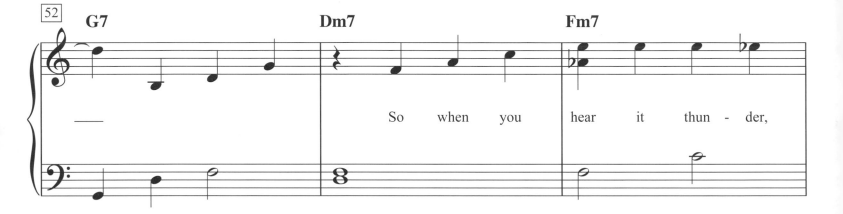

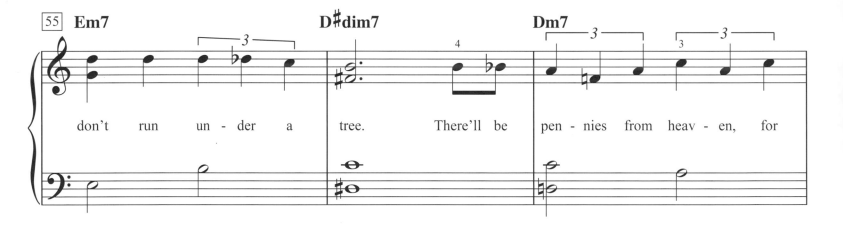

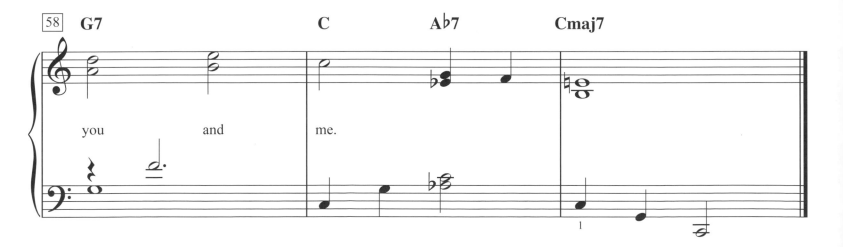

Pick Yourself Up

from SWING TIME

Words by DOROTHY FIELDS
Music by JEROME KERN

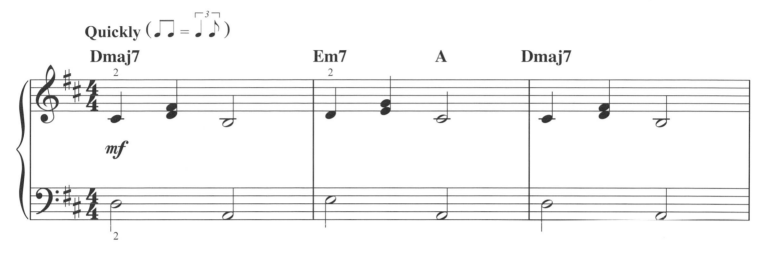

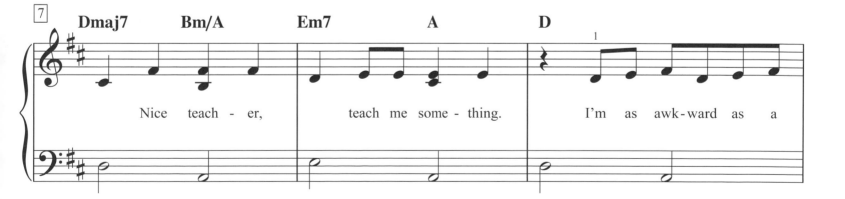

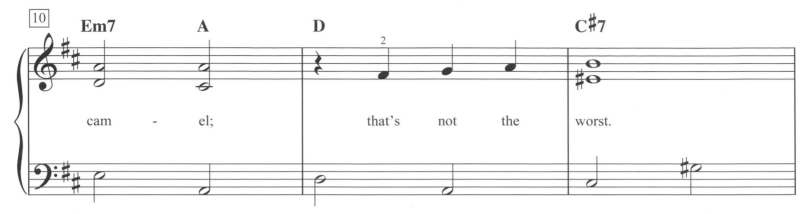

cam - el; that's not the worst.

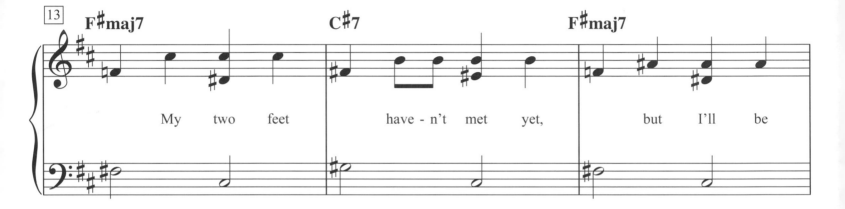

My two feet have-n't met yet, but I'll be

teach-er's pet yet, 'cause I'm gon-na learn to dance or

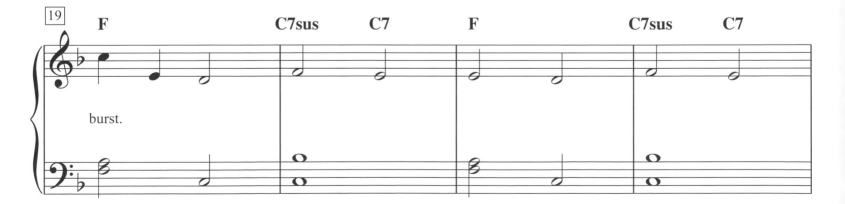

burst.

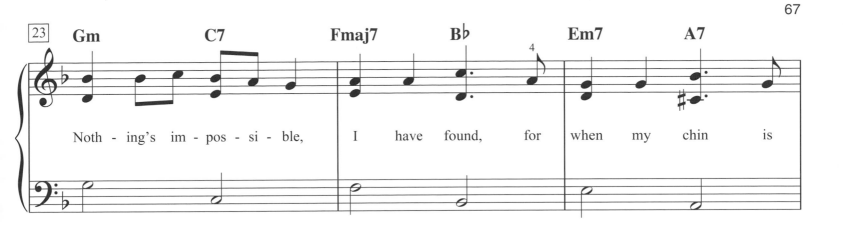

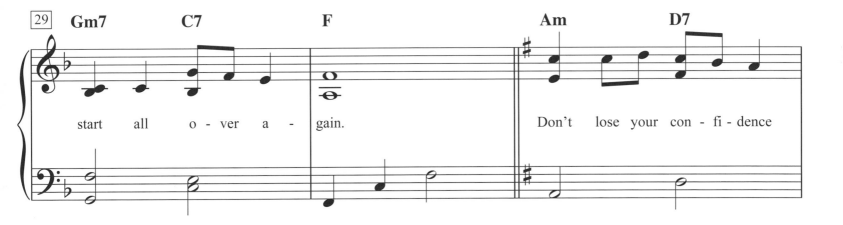

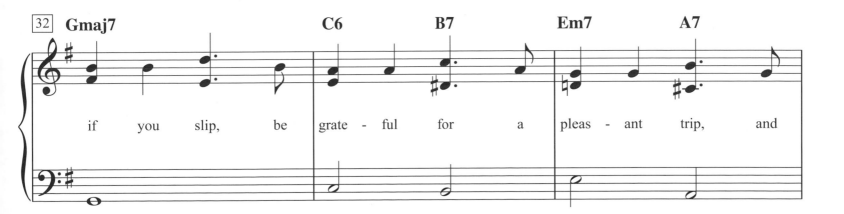

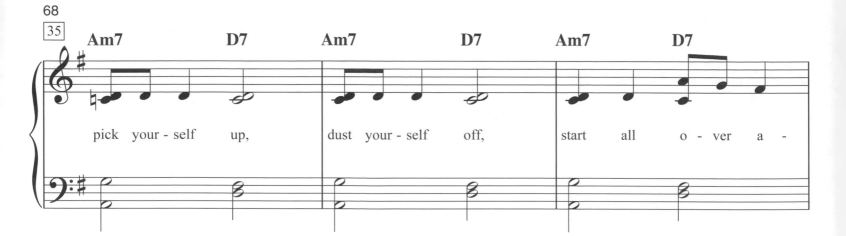

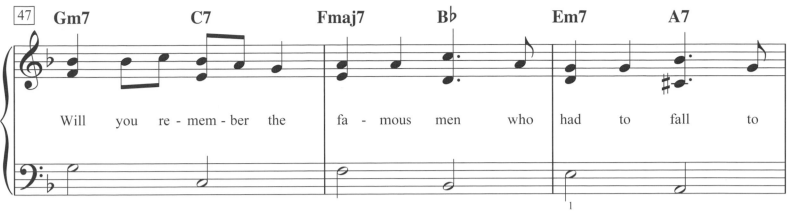

Will you re-mem-ber the fa-mous men who had to fall to

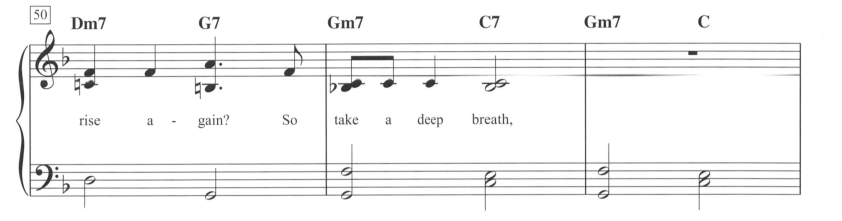

rise a - gain? So take a deep breath,

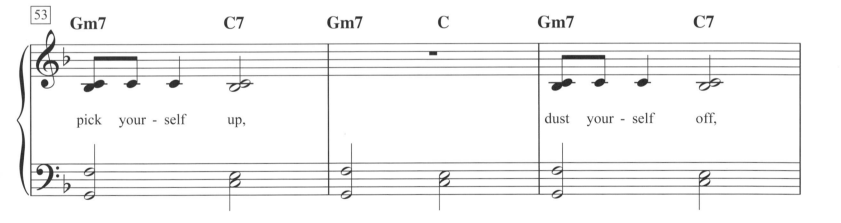

pick your-self up, dust your-self off,

start all o-ver a - gain.

Put On a Happy Face

from BYE BYE BIRDIE

Lyric by LEE ADAMS
Music by CHARLES STROUSE

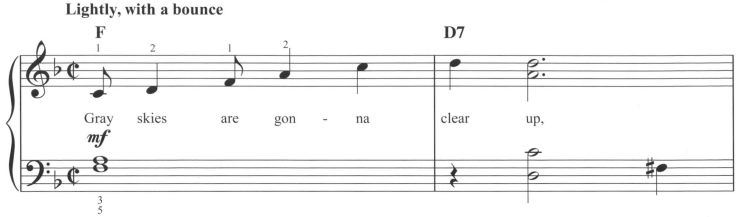

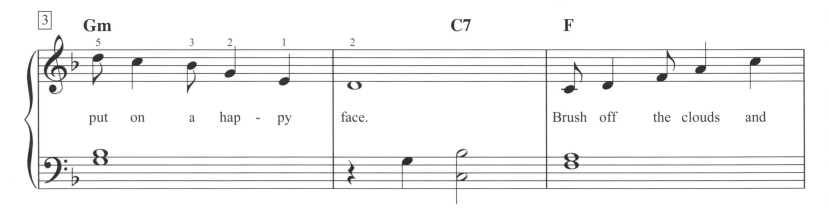

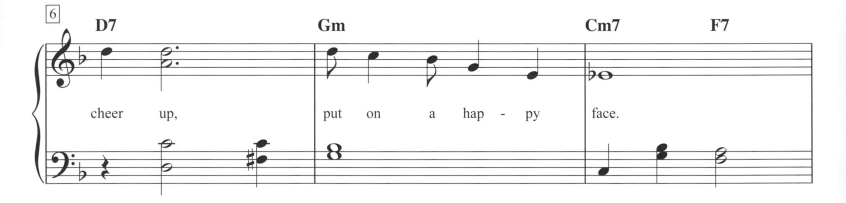

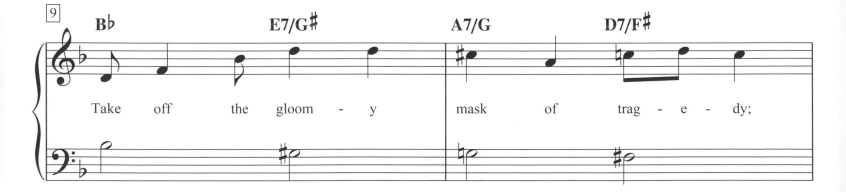

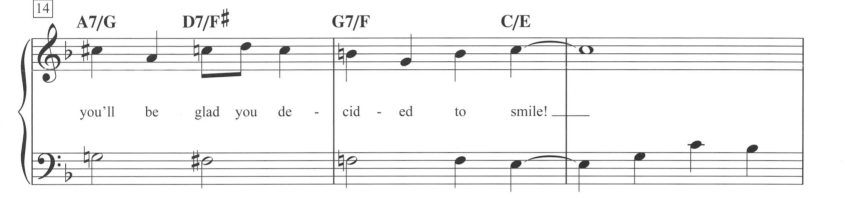

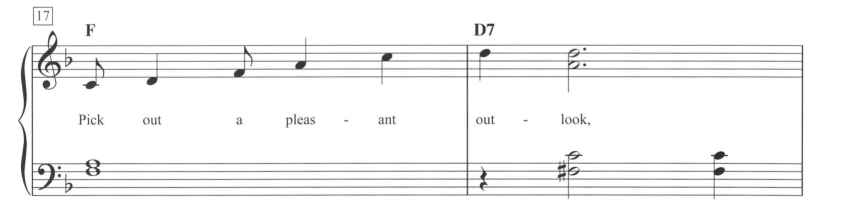

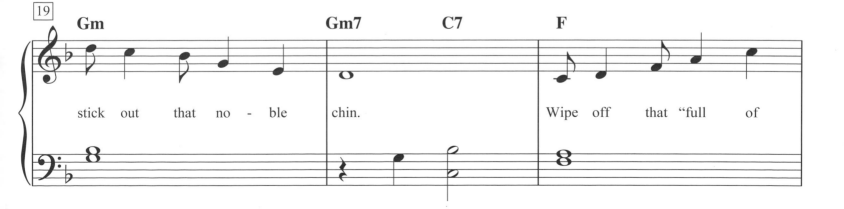

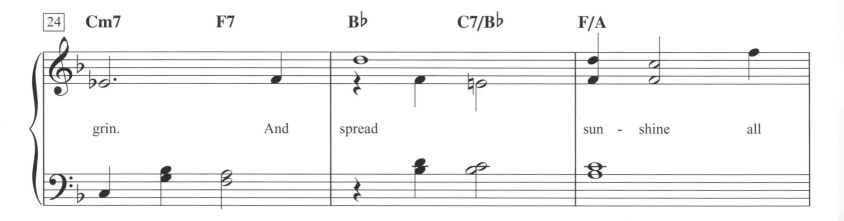

Summertime

from PORGY AND BESS®

Music and Lyrics by GEORGE GERSHWIN,
DuBOSE and DOROTHY HEYWARD
and IRA GERSHWIN

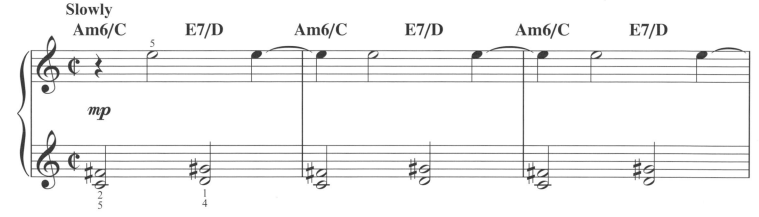

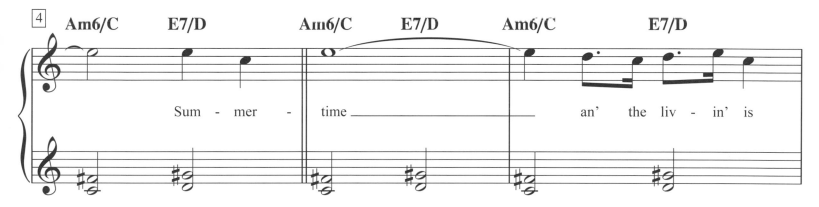

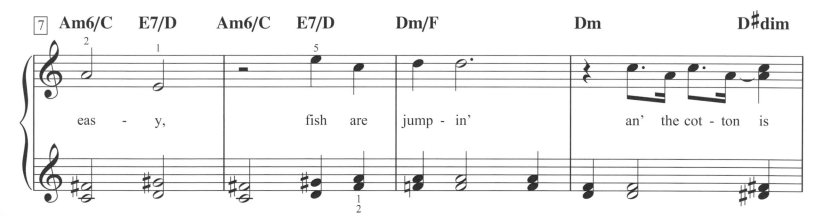

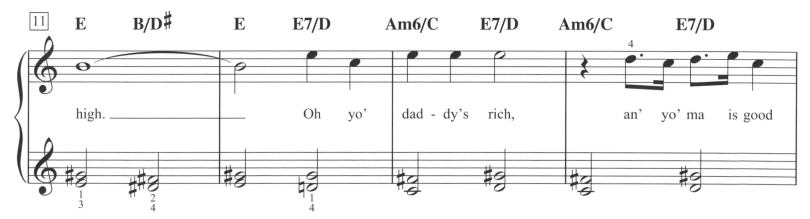

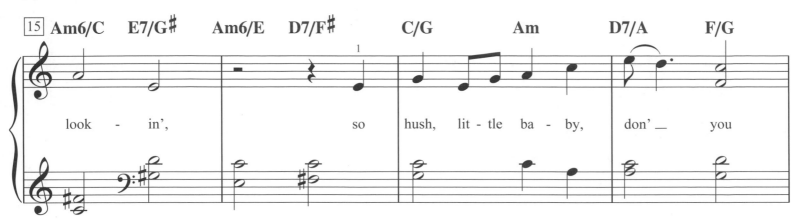

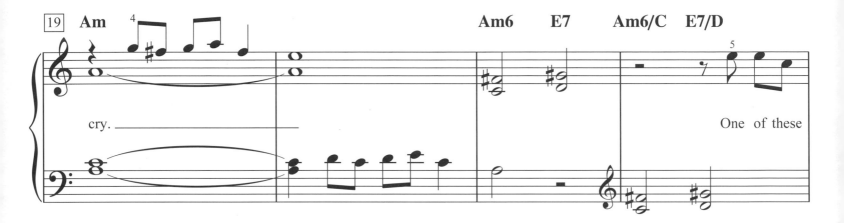

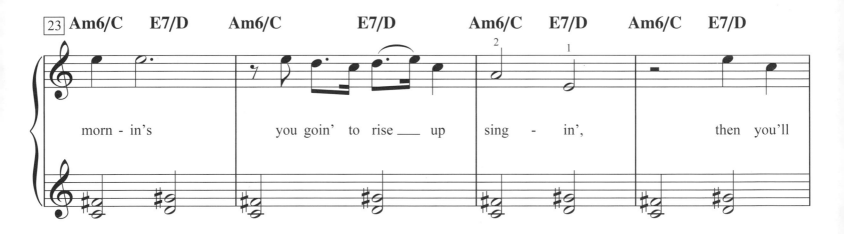

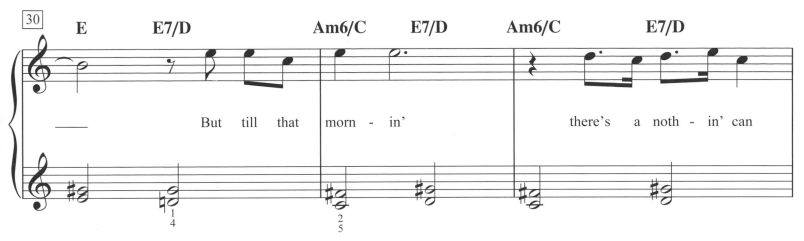

But till that morn - in'   there's a noth - in' can

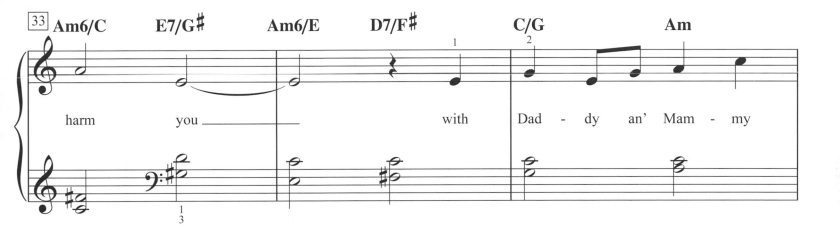

harm you _____   with Dad - dy an' Mam - my

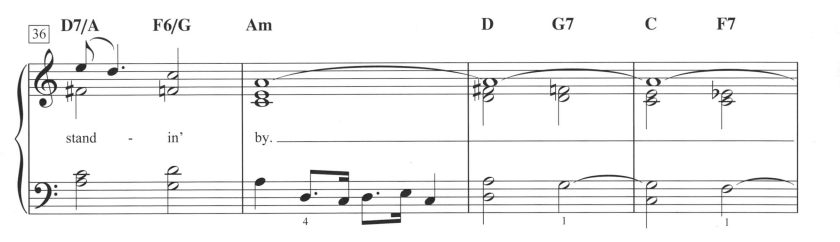

stand - in'   by. _____

rit.

Sweet Georgia Brown

Words and Music by BEN BERNIE
MACEO PINKARD and KENNETH CASEY

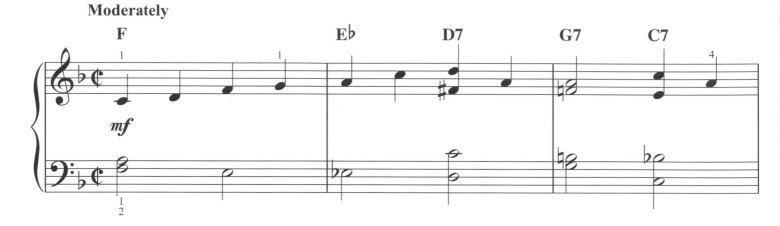

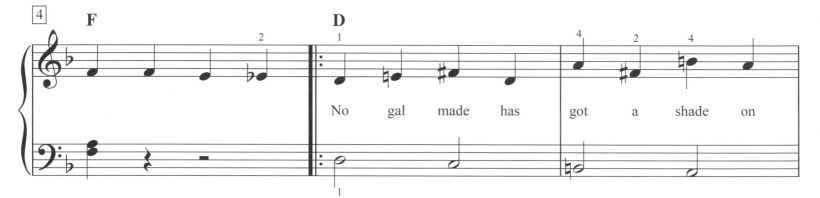

No gal made has got a shade on

sweet Geor - gia Brown, _____ two left feet but

oh so neat has sweet Geor - gia Brown. _____

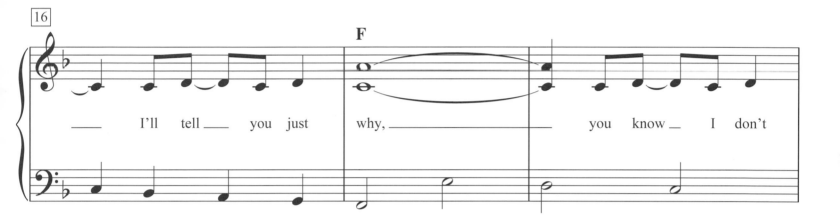

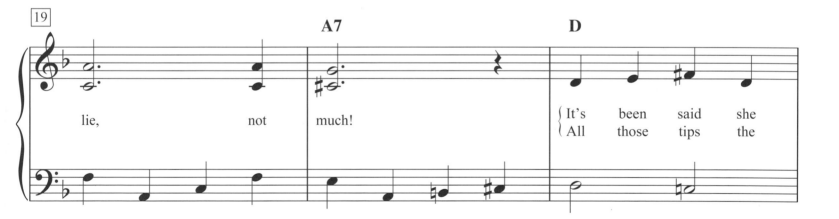

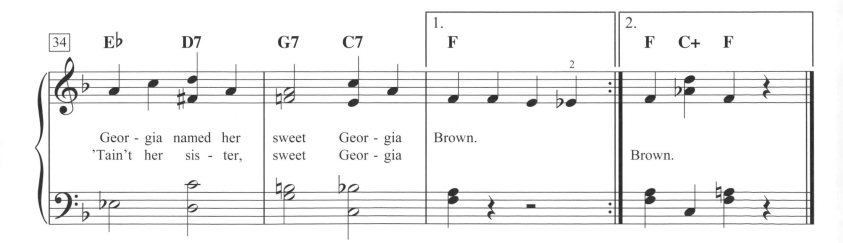

Take the "A" Train

Words and Music by
BILLY STRAYHORN

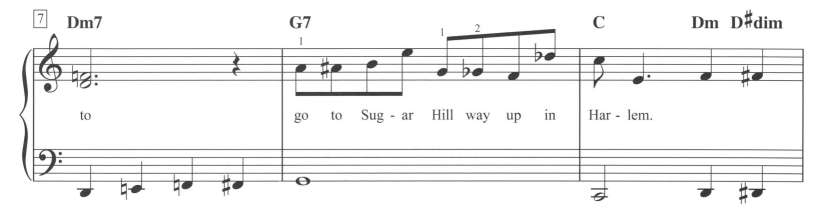

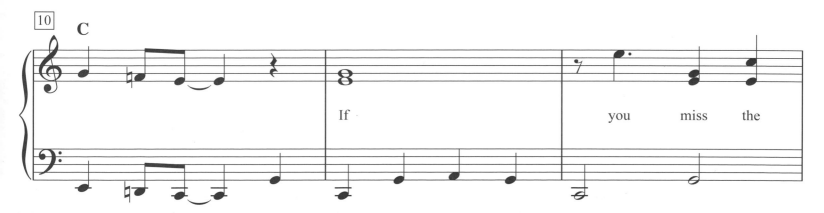

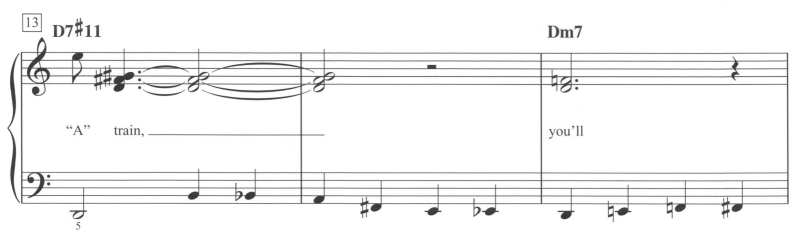

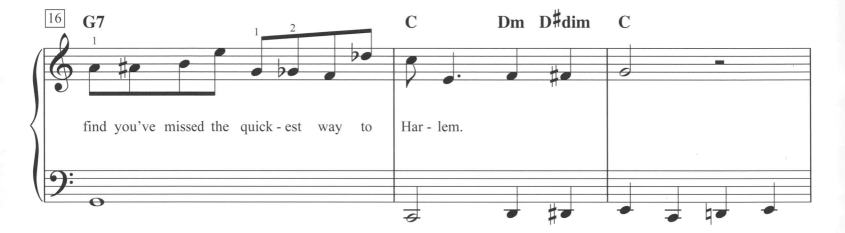

What a Wonderful World

Words and Music by GEORGE DAVID WEISS
and BOB THIELE

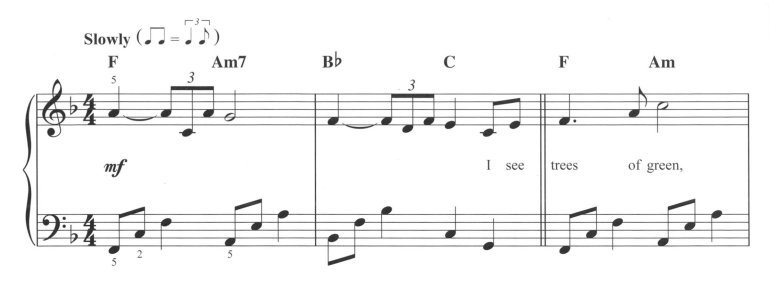

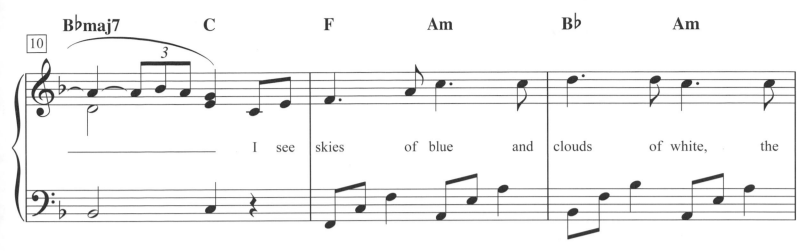

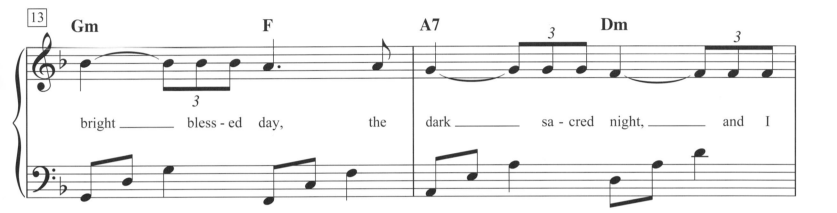

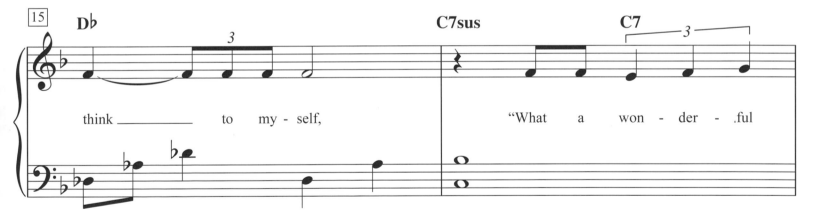

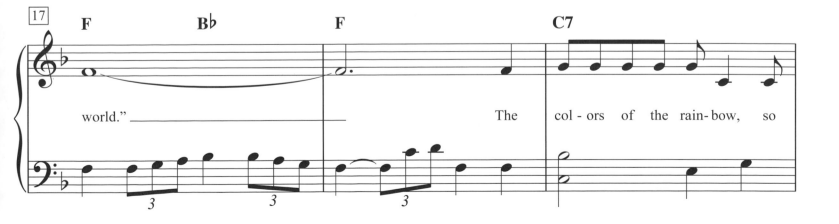

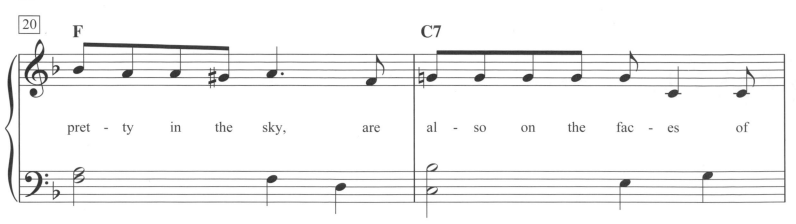

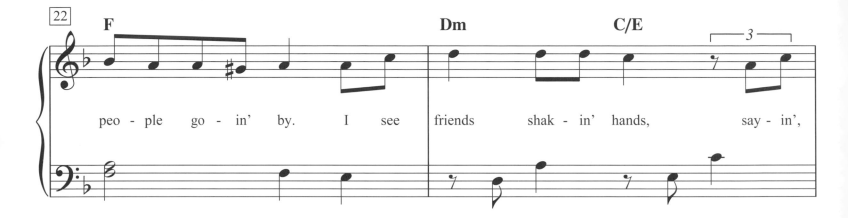

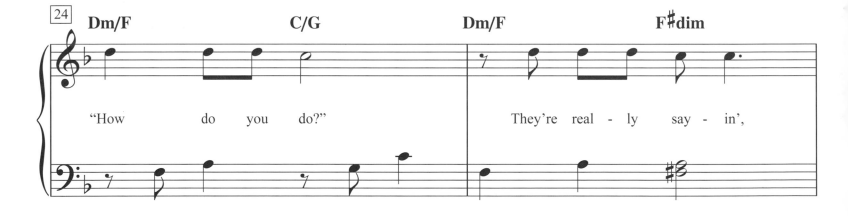

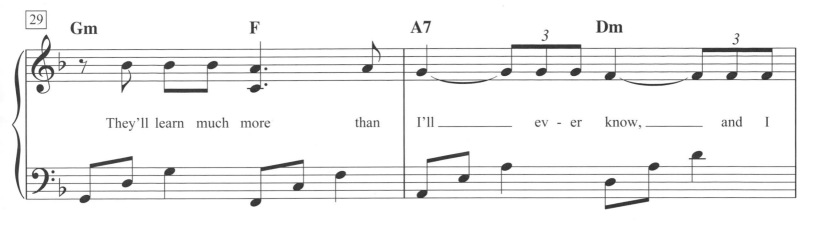

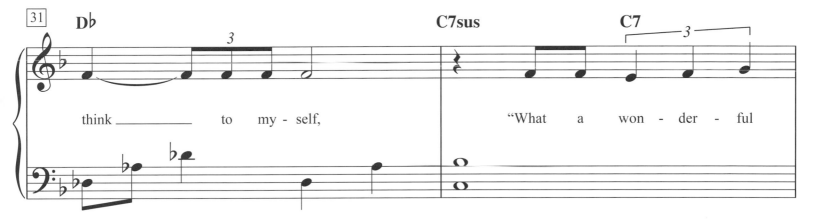

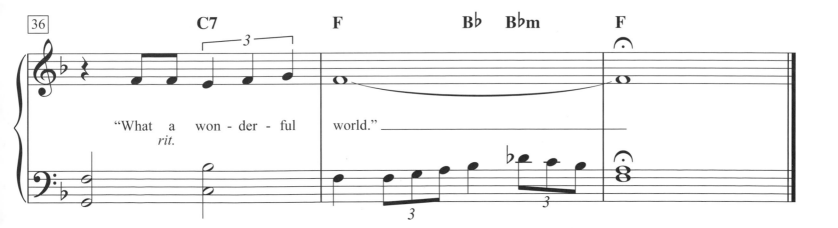

A-Tisket A-Tasket

Words and Music by ELLA FITZGERALD
and VAN ALEXANDER

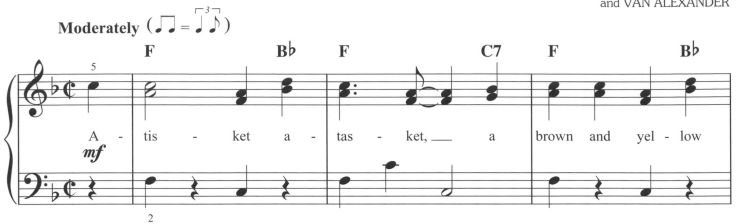

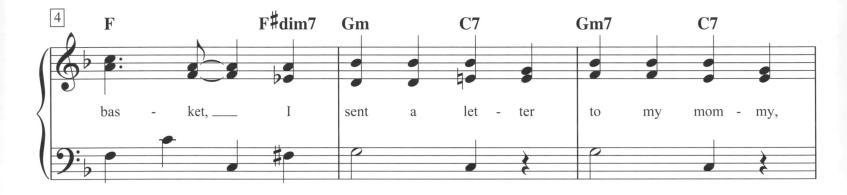

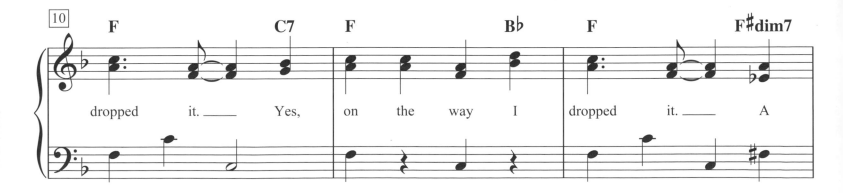

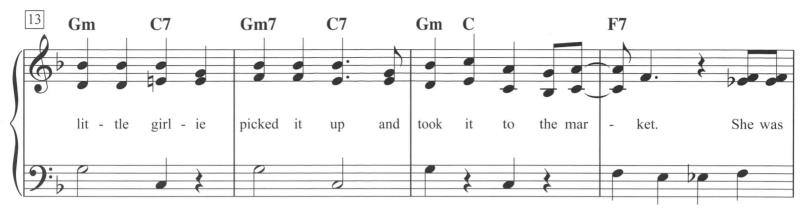

lit - tle girl - ie picked it up and took it to the mar - ket. She was

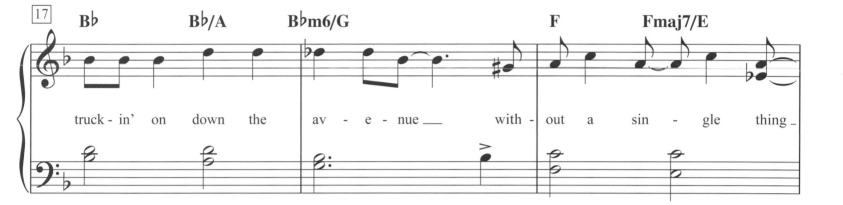

truck - in' on down the av - e - nue __ with - out a sin - gle thing __

__ to do. __ She was peck, peck, peck - in' all a - round, __

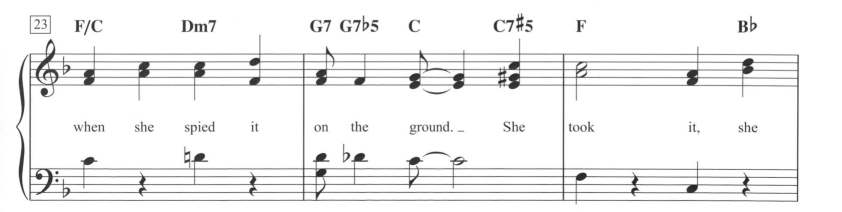

when she spied it on the ground. __ She took it, she

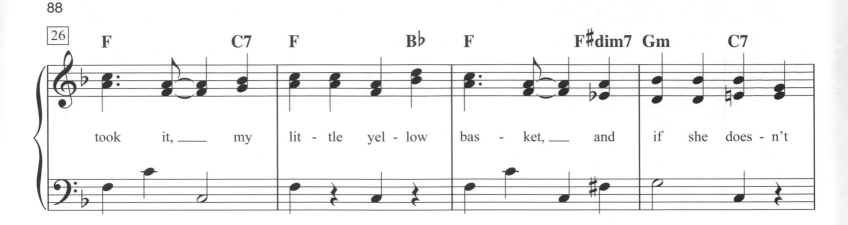